LLYWELYN THE GREAT
Prince of Gwynedd

LLYWELYN THE GREAT

Prince of Gwynedd

Roger Turvey

Gomer

Published in 2007 by
Gomer Press, Llandysul, Ceredigion, SA44 4JL

ISBN 978 1 84323 747 1

A CIP record for this title is available from the British Library.

This book is published with the financial support of the
Welsh Books Council.

Printed and bound in Wales at
Gomer Press, Llandysul, Ceredigion

For my daughters

Siân Eleri and Aranwen Jane

ACKNOWLEDGEMENTS

I am grateful to Professor Emeritus Ralph Griffiths for reading and commenting on this book. His characteristically generous support, encouragement and advice over the years are very much appreciated. Needless to say, the responsibility for any errors or other deficiencies in the book is mine alone.

I am indebted to William Rees's *An Historical Atlas of Wales*, R.R. Davies's *Conquest, Coexistence and Change Wales 1063–1415*, Richard Avent's *Castles of the Princes of Gwynedd*, and Neil Johnstone's 'Llys and Maerdref: the Royal Courts of the Princes of Gwynedd', *Studia Celtica*, XXXIV, for much of the information included in my own maps.

I am particularly grateful to my colleague, Einir Jones, for putting her expertise in Welsh poetry at my disposal. I wish to thank Ceri Wyn Jones and Gomer Press for their willingness to take on this project and bring it to fruition.

I would also like to thank the friends and colleagues with whom I have discussed parts of this book, but my greatest debt is to my wife and fellow historian Carol for her sound advice and unfailing support.

CONTENTS

PREFACE

The primary aim of this book is to provide a synthesis of the history of, arguably, the most important, if not the greatest, native ruler in pre-conquest Wales. By incorporating the results of recent scholarship, the book seeks to provide the reader with a relatively brief and generally broad-ranging introduction to the life and career of Llywelyn ap Iorwerth, which, it need hardly be stressed, is deserving of further and more detailed study. Though modest, this short, popular study has the virtue of being the first publication to focus specifically on Llywelyn the Great, providing for the first time a scholarly overview of his activities and his contribution to the history of medieval Wales.

The importance of princes like Llywelyn in the history of Wales cannot be overstated. Their capacity to shape and influence the political, social, religious, cultural and economic developments in their respective territories is suggestive of an impact that simply cannot be ignored. The extent to which they have earned the attention of historians is made manifest in the titular currency afforded by such as 'The Age of the Princes' and the 'Wales of the Princes'. Indeed, in the opinion of Sir John Edward Lloyd, one of Wales's finest medieval historians, the thirteenth century itself may be described as the 'age of the two Llywelyns'. This 'princely' period in Welsh medieval history has been described as an 'epoch', which came to an end with the Edwardian conquest of 1282-3. That they have lent themselves to describing an 'age' and an 'epoch' in the history of Wales points unmistakably to their importance and their worth as a subject of study.

The truly 'great' princes are those who to some degree succeeded in transcending their times and, with an eye for power and profit, ruthlessly took advantage of their opportunities. They are also those princes most likely to be celebrated in song by bards, referenced in official records by clerks and referred to in chronicles by monastic scribes. Consequently, in the period between 1066 and 1283, it is, arguably, only possible to highlight the achievements of no more than half a dozen princes, the

majority of whom hail from Gwynedd, among them Gruffudd ap
Cynan (d.1137), Owain (Gwynedd) ap Gruffudd (d.1170),
Llywelyn ap Iorwerth (d.1240) and Llywelyn ap Gruffudd
(d.1282). Of these, Llywelyn ap Iorwerth alone is remembered
today as 'the Great', a title that posterity saw fit to bestow upon
him decades after his death.

It was his determination, courage and selfish desire to rule that
enabled a prince of Gwynedd to unite much of Wales politically.
This was without doubt Llywelyn's greatest achievement, for in
setting the standard and in establishing the precedent he enabled
his grandson, Llywelyn ap Gruffudd, to turn theory into reality.

ABBREVIATIONS

Ann. Camb.	*Annales Cambriae*, ed. J. Williams ab Ithel (Rolls Series, 1860).
Autobiog.	Butler, H.E., *The Autobiography of Giraldus Cambrensis* (Rev. edn., Woodbridge, 2005).
AWR	Pryce, Huw (ed.). *The Acts of Welsh Rulers, 1120-1283* (Cardiff, 2005).
BBCS	*Bulletin of the Board of Celtic Studies.*
BT.Pen.	*Brut y Tywysogyon or The Chronicle of the Princes. Peniarth Ms 20 Version.* Translated with introduction and notes by Thomas Jones (Cardiff, 1952).
BT.RBH.	*Brut y Tywysogyon or The Chronicle of the Princes. Red Book of Hergest Version.* Translated with introduction and notes by Thomas Jones (Cardiff, 1955).
B. Saes.	*Brenhinedd y Saesson or The Kings of the Saxons.* Translated with introduction and notes by Thomas Jones (Cardiff, 1971).
CAC	*Calendar of Ancient Correspondence concerning Wales.* Edited by J.G. Edwards (Cardiff, 1935).
Carr, *MW*	Carr, A.D., *Medieval Wales* (1995).
DWB	Lloyd, J. E.; Jenkins, R. T.; Davies, W. L., Sir; Davies, M. B. (ed.). *The Dictionary of Welsh Biography down to 1940* (Cardiff, 1959).
CW	'Cronica de Wallia and other documents from Exeter Cathedral Library MS. 3514', ed. T. Jones, *BBCS*, 12 (1946-8).
EHR	*English History Review.*
Litt. Wallie	*Littere Wallie preserved in Liber A in the Public Record Office.* Edited with introduction by J.G. Edwards (Cardiff, 1940).
Lloyd, *HW*	Lloyd, J.E., *A History of Wales from Earliest Times to the Edwardian Conquest* (2 vols, London, 1911).
THSC	*Transactions of the Honourable Society of Cymmrodorion.*
TRHS	*Transactions of the Royal Historical Society.*
WHR	*Welsh History Review.*

List of Genealogical Tables, Illustrations and Maps

Regional and local divisions of Medieval Wales.

I

Introduction:
Background and Sources

The history of Wales in the two centuries between the coming of the Normans in 1066 and the Edwardian conquest in 1282-3 is essentially the history of its rulers. This book is about a ruler who, by his statesmanship and soldiery came to dominate the political life of medieval Wales. It is not possible, even if it is desirable, to write a full biography of a medieval person, even someone as powerful as Llywelyn the Great.[1] In the cases of those individual rulers who were written about, we may have a general idea of their character but little in terms of their personal appearance. There are no portraits, no death masks and no contemporary tomb effigy of Llywelyn but even if there were, they would need to be treated with circumspection, since it was customary to portray important figures as it was thought they ought to look, rather than as they actually were.[2] This applies equally to written descriptions and contemporary estimations, particularly those penned by the bards and poets, which tend to portray their subjects in an idealized way. Consequently, much of what we learn about Llywelyn comes to us by means of what he did and how he did it. It is why and how he reacted to events, pressures and problems that offer the best insight into what he was like.

Land, lordship and local acknowledgement were among the key determinants of a ruler's status but war was his badge of honour. The native rulers were a warrior elite who, unlike the majority of their subjects whose social and political horizon was bounded by the structures of local life – the village, its church and the seigneur – took a broader view of the world that involved kingships and kingdoms. By a process of expansion, definition and development, particularly in the agencies of coercive authority, they worked towards creating coherent

territorial entities, polities that were described variously as
kingdoms or principalities. The more successful rulers were those
who were able effectively to wield power, not just over the bond
or peasant element of the population, but over the free or noble
element also. By attempting to create an administrative
infrastructure for their respective polities, they were attempting
to make real and tangible their power and authority. The
exceptional among them succeeded in broadening their power by
exercising a form of hegemony over the other native rulers of
Wales. As his singular appellation suggests, Llywelyn 'the Great'
was among the more successful and exceptional of these native
rulers.

THE WALES OF LLYWELYN

> Cambria is called Wales . . . It is two hundred miles long and
> about one hundred miles wide. It takes some eight days to
> travel the whole length, from the mouth of the River Gwygir
> in Anglesey to Portskewett in Gwent. In breadth it stretches
> from Porth-mawr, that is the Great Port, near St. David's, to
> Rhyd-helyg, the Welsh for Willow Ford, called Walford in
> English, this being a journey which lasts four days. Because of
> its high mountains, deep valleys and extensive forests, not to
> mention its rivers and marches, it is not easy of access.[3]

Thus was Wales described by one who knew it well. Writing
in the last decade of the twelfth century, Gerald de Barri, or as he
is most commonly known, Gerald of Wales, had not long
completed a journey through a land in which he was born
and which he proudly called home. Nor was his knowledge
confined simply to the geography of Wales; he knew much of its
often bloody history and the resulting political divisions of the
country:

> From time immemorial Wales has been divided into three
> more or less equal parts. When I say equal I mean in value
> rather than in size. These are Gwynedd, or North Wales; South

Wales, called in Welsh Deheubarth, which really means Right-Hand Wales; and Powys, which is the middle and stretches eastwards.[4]

Although he was of mixed race, Anglo-Norman and Welsh, and had been brought up in the Anglo-Norman colony of south Pembrokeshire, he knew well some of the ruling princes of his day, one of whom, the Lord Rhys, Prince of Deheubarth, he called cousin. Unfortunately for us, Gerald did not know Llywelyn as well as he did Rhys, but he did meet with him, perhaps on his journey through Gwynedd in 1188, but certainly for some four days in 1202. There may have been other occasions when the two met, but they have escaped the chronicler's pen, but it is certain the two corresponded and kept in touch via intermediaries.

In his twin-treatise on Wales and the Welsh, appropriately entitled *The Journey through Wales* and *The Description of*

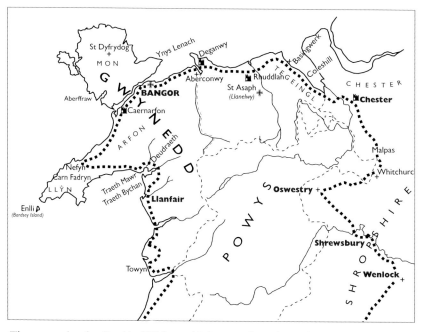

The route taken by Gerald of Wales on his journey through north Wales in 1188.

Wales, Gerald admits that the Wales of his time is hard to define. Its territorial extent varied according to the ebb and flow of war, so that its shape was largely dictated by invasion, conquest, and settlement. This had as much to do with aggressive Anglo-Saxon and later Norman and Anglo-Norman conquerors as with the Welsh themselves for they were a divided people and, in a land where local and regional identities were strong, prone to violent dispute.

It was a land of multiple-kingship, which because of its high mountains, deep valleys and extensive forests, not to mention its rivers and marshes, did not make for unified control or a unified development. Thus, for example, the Wales encountered by Gerald on his journey in 1188 consisted of a number of separate kingdoms which varied considerably in size and strength, but each of which had its territorial identity, cultural traditions, ruling dynasty and, most precious of all, its independence. Consequently, unlike its near neighbour England, Wales did not, until later and principally during the reign of Llywelyn ap Iorwerth, experience that process of political coalescence that might lead to the emergence of a single kingdom and kingship.

Sadly, Gerald is largely silent on the politics of Gwynedd and the means by which Llywelyn rose to and later seized power in that kingdom. Nor is he as forthcoming on a fulsome description of Gwynedd as he was wont to present on Deheubarth. Indeed, as if to emphasize his southern Welsh credentials, Gerald spent nearly five of his seven-week journey around Wales and the border region (2 March – 23 April 1188) in the south. In stark contrast, his journey through north Wales was accomplished in a week of hard travelling. As a consequence, it is not possible to do for Gwynedd what Huw Pryce managed to do for Deheubarth in his article 'In search of a medieval society: Deheubarth in the writings of Gerald of Wales', in which he succeeded in capturing something of the complexity and variety of its 'social and economic life' through the 'richness and diversity of Gerald's literary output'.[5] It is perhaps unfair to criticise Gerald for his ignorance of Gwynedd for, as Huw Pryce pointed out, he was 'very much a stranger in the north'.[6] Nevertheless, what Gerald has to say about Gwynedd, particularly during his visit to preach and recruit for the crusade in 1188, is worth recording if only for the light it sheds on the land known to and claimed by Llywelyn in his youth.

Gerald and his party of fellow crusading preachers, who included Baldwin, the Archbishop of Canterbury, set foot in Gwynedd on 7 April 1188 when they crossed the river Dyfi. In fact, the rivers of north Wales made an impression on Gerald as did 'the awesome nature of the land itself'.[7] He mentions the crossings by boat of the Dyfi, Mawddach, Conwy and Dee, along with the sea crossings from Eifionydd to Llŷn near modern-day Porthmadog, and from Bangor to Anglesey. However, it was the mountain peaks of Snowdonia that caught Gerald's eye for they 'are thought to be so enormous and to extend so far that [they] seem to rear their lofty summits right up to the clouds'.[8] Moreover, he was convinced that 'if all the herds were gathered together, Snowdon could afford sufficient pasture.'[9] He was less impressed with the Cader Idris range where, in his opinion, 'the mountains are very high, with narrow ridges and a great number of very sharp peaks all jumbled together in confusion.'[10] Indeed, Gerald found Meirionnydd to be among the 'rudest and roughest of all the Welsh districts', an opinion shared by a fellow traveller, Joseph Hucks, who passed through 'the wildest and most desolate country that North Wales can boast of' a little over six hundred years later in July 1794.[11]

Gerald was equally unimpressed with Anglesey which he likened to 'the cantref of Pebidiog, round St David's' being a somewhat 'arid stony land, rough and unattractive in appearance.'[12] That said, he was full of praise for the island's fertility and 'natural productivity' especially in the production of grain, which he believed could 'supply all Wales'. It was precisely because of what Gerald describes in a moment of contradiction as the 'richness of its soil and its abundant produce' that Anglesey was so valuable to the rulers of Gwynedd who acknowledged its importance by siting the chief court of the kingdom at Aberffraw.[13] Gerald did not visit Aberffraw during this journey though he might have done fourteen years later, in 1202, when he met Llywelyn. In fact, at no point during his visit to north Wales did he describe, let alone acknowledge, the existence of the regional courts (*llysoedd*), such as at Aber and Caernarfon, even though he must have passed by or through them. Nor did Gerald refer to any native boroughs such as at Nefyn, which was established some time before 1200 and where he preached and spent the third night of his journey.

Fortunately, the castles, cathedral towns and monasteries of north Wales were noted by Gerald, though they too seem not to have impressed him. Certainly the castles of Deudraeth and Carn Fadryn were worthy of note only because they were among the first to be built in stone by the north Welsh. Rhuddlan, 'a fine castle on the river Clwyd', merited Gerald's attention though he does not elaborate other than to say that he was 'suitably entertained that night' within its walls by its keeper, Llywelyn's uncle, Dafydd ab Owain. The cathedral town of St Asaph was described as 'small' while Bangor elicited no description other than his having seen the tombs of Owain Gwynedd (d.1170) and his brother Cadwaladr (d.1172) within the cathedral there. Would that Gerald had said more about the industrial development of Gwynedd which is dismissed in a single intriguing sentence: 'We passed through a district where there [were] successful mining-works, and where, by delving deep, "They penetrate the very bowels of the earth".'[14]

Gerald's last night in north Wales was spent at the 'small priory at Basingwerk' near Holywell, after which he traversed, 'not without considerable apprehension' the 'extensive quicksand' that lay between him and the ford on the river Dee that led to Chester. It is worth noting that before leaving Gwynedd he was keen to relate his coming across 'a rich vein of silver' somewhere between St Asaph and Basingwerk.[15]

Having forded rivers by foot and by boat, crossed quicksand, passed by densely wooded districts and ridden along the coast between sea and steep cliffs, Gerald has left us with a picture of Gwynedd which in part explains why it proved so difficult to conquer. If, as a peaceful traveller, Gerald found that the 'going was hard, with many steep climbs up and down', how much more formidable and dangerous the terrain must have appeared to a potential aggressor. The fact that Gerald and his party were regularly forced to dismount and proceed on foot again highlights the difficulties experienced by invading English armies, particularly those ill-fated expeditions led by Henry II against Llywelyn's grandfather, Owain Gwynedd, in 1157 and 1165. Gwynedd's geographical strength may also be considered a source of potential weakness for if it was a difficult kingdom to attack it was equally difficult to control and govern. As David Stephenson pointed out, 'these same obstacles to the stranger served to make internal communications a difficult undertaking for the native ruler.'[16] The fact that Llywelyn ap Iorwerth succeeded in overcoming these obstacles to make Gwynedd the most powerful and seemingly well governed kingdom in the land is a testimony to his special talents as a ruler.

POLITICAL BACKGROUND

In terms of their size, strength and longevity, the most powerful kingdoms in twelfth-century Wales were, according to Gerald of Wales, Gwynedd, Powys and Deheubarth. Of these Gwynedd alone emerged enlarged and powerful enough to dominate the Welsh political landscape in the thirteenth century. For much of the two centuries after 1066, the rulers of these kingdoms, including the minor lords of territories like Arwystli, Gwrtheyrnion, Elfael and Maelienydd were selfishly engaged in their own almost endless political and military conflicts. Rulers and kingdoms vied with each other for supremacy, pursuing objectives that were, for the most part, instinctual. It was, in part, a Wales manufactured by war, fashioned by the ambitions of rulers bent on uniting under their command the territories of their dissident native neighbours whom they sought to make their vassals.

Thus did successive rulers of Gwynedd make war on their rivals, the rulers of Deheubarth and Powys, in order to conquer and annex territory. Consequently, by the thirteenth century, Wales had at its territorial core the kingdom of Gwynedd and at its political heart a prince of Gwynedd. It was a Wales united less by idealism, much less the anachronism of nationalism, than by conquest and coercion. Nor was this competition for power confined to rivalry between kingdoms but rather involved dynastic struggles within kingdoms also: between 949 and 1066 no fewer than thirty-five rulers were butchered at the hands of their compatriots. Only when there emerged a leader of exceptional authority and skill could a kingdom transcend this internal violence and make its mark on the wider political stage. The twin elements of territorial fluidity and political fragility ensured that political unity was invariably transient and ephemeral, and was most likely to be achieved by military might alone.

On occasion, the balance of power in this fragmented land turned on the intervention of English kings, who were concerned to maintain Welsh recognition of their hegemony without necessarily having to enforce it physically. At no time before the reign of Edward I (1272-1307) did the Crown seriously contemplate the conquest of Wales (though King John came closest) being content to demonstrate its power by means of spasmodic, and occasionally impressive, military expeditions. In all, twenty-one royal expeditions were launched in Wales between 1081 and 1267, some of the more successful being those led by John (1199-1216) in 1211 and Henry III (1216-72) in 1241. Apart from their dynastic wrangling, royal intervention generally caused the native rulers their greatest turmoil, in that they almost inevitably led to disruption and destruction or, in some instances, their demotion, and in the worst cases, even their deaths. Equally tumultuous were the periods when royal rule was at its weakest, as in the reign of Stephen (1135-54), at its most indifferent as in the reign of Richard I (1189-99), or at its most distracted, as it was for short periods in the reigns John and Henry III. These periods enabled the more enterprising Welsh rulers to reshape, to their advantage, the map of political power in Wales.

The Crown's occasional interest in Welsh affairs before the mid-to late thirteenth century meant that the balance of power in Wales was more often likely to depend on the emergence of outstandingly able or ruthless native and Marcher leaders. The capture of large swathes of Welsh territory by the Marcher barons serves to highlight the new and permanent element that was introduced to the history of Wales by the coming of the Normans. These barons and knights were intent on carving out for themselves territorial enclaves in this region of the Anglo-Welsh frontier or March. The Marchers' free-enterprise, land-grabbing expeditions along coasts and river valleys, staking their claim by erecting earth and timber castles as they went, transformed the power structure in Wales. By dint of their conquests, the eastern and southern parts of Wales were occupied by Marcher lordships that ranged in size from great earldoms like Pembroke and Glamorgan to lesser entities like Builth and Gower. Indeed, great Marcher families like Braose, Clare, Marshal and Mortimer were no whit less dynastic in outlook than their native counterparts with whom they contended for control of Wales. It was the conflict arising from this political, territorial and jurisdictional division between Marcher lords and native rulers, a pattern that was to last, in its basic outlines, throughout the twelfth century and for most of the thirteenth, that provided the native rulers, who had constantly to live on the edge of conquest, with some of their sternest challenges.

A country geographically and politically fragmented did not make for easy internal communication and in the absence of an accessible heartland that might serve as a focus for unity, it was almost inevitable that loyalties would be intensely local. That said there is sufficient evidence from contemporary literature to suggest that the Welsh were self-aware and that they tended to express their sense of identity by looking back to the past when, as 'Britons', their ancestors had ruled the whole island of Britain. In the opinion of Michael Richter, it is in the two centuries before the Edwardian conquest of 1282-3 that the Welsh people 'experienced an enlargement of their view of the world, when gradually they came to know each other as fellow-countrymen by being fellow-sufferers.'[17] Their coming together was indeed a slow and painful process, made harder by the petty squabbling that not only marked relations between the nation's political leaders, but marred family relationships within their respective dynasties.

After 1066 two rulers only succeeded in extending their hegemony over the greater part of Wales: Llywelyn ap Iorwerth (1216-1240) and his grandson Llywelyn ap Gruffudd (1258-82). That both hailed from Gwynedd reveals the extent to which this kingdom realised its potential to become the most powerful element in Welsh dynastic politics. The key to the success of the two Llywelyns, besides their military muscle, was bringing to heel the other native rulers within a political framework that tolerated but excluded the Marcher lords, whilst simultaneously seeking acknowledgement by the English Crown of their status as undisputed masters within a separate and unitary principality. Co-existence and co-operation with their Marcher neighbours and royal overlords became as much a feature of their policies as conflict and conquest had been. Consequently, under their capable and enlightened leadership, the prospect of creating a united native polity gradually turned into a practical proposition during the latter half of Llywelyn ap Iorwerth's reign and was, briefly, realised in that of his grandson Llywelyn ap Gruffudd between 1267 and 1277.

It is fair to say that the credit for establishing Gwynedd's primacy in Welsh affairs is due, primarily, to the work of two earlier rulers, Gruffudd ap Cynan (c.1075-1137) and his son Owain ap Gruffudd or, as he is most commonly known, Owain Gwynedd (1137-70). They withstood the external pressures of Marcher ambition and royal intervention whilst repairing the dynastic fissures that regularly threatened to tear their rule and territorial power apart. They ruled, according to one contemporary chronicler, 'with an iron rod'[18] so that, between them, they created a stable and prosperous kingdom by strengthening their hold on church and state and by wisely acknowledging English suzerainty. They were also responsible for originating and promoting the idea that a ruler of Gwynedd possessed authority over Wales as a whole, and, as if to emphasize the fact of their primacy, to Owain Gwynedd goes the credit of being among the first of his countrymen to cultivate a diplomatic friendship with a foreign ruler, Louis VII of France (1137-80).

SOURCES

The Welsh ruling elite of pre-conquest Wales are more elusive than their English or continental counterparts. Chronologically, geographically and familially, the sources simply do not have a great deal to say about the medieval rulers of Wales much before the thirteenth century, or much beyond the borders and dynasty of Gwynedd. Consequently, much of the scholarly activity directed at the Princes, certainly since the publication of Sir John Edward Lloyd's classic *A History of Wales from the Earliest Times to the Edwardian Conquest* (1911), has been confined to articles in learned journals or the short book. This is not to suggest that Welsh 'princely' studies is a neglected field, far from it. As recently as 2003, Charles Insley was moved to declare that the reign of Llywelyn ap Iorwerth is 'one of the most studied periods in Welsh history.'[19] Although this might be a touch exaggerated, it well reflects the attention that historians have paid in print to the princes, both individually and collectively, in the last thirty-five years. Nevertheless, it is true to say that Llywelyn ap Gruffudd alone, the last native ruler of a largely united Wales, has been able to command sufficient source material for the kind of book, over 600 pages, that is relatively commonplace on chronologically comparable rulers in England such as Henry III and Edward I. Indeed, it is unlikely that books on this scale can or will be written on individual Welsh princes which is why some scholars have adopted a new approach, namely, the collaborative biography. This technique has resulted in separate studies of two twelfth-century rulers, Gruffudd ap Cynan of Gwynedd and, in Welsh, Rhys ap Gruffudd of Deheubarth.

The principal narrative source for the history of the Welsh princes is the *Brut y Tywysogyon* or *The Chronicle of the Princes*. Compiled sometime in the second half of the thirteenth-century by anonymous monastic scribes and copyists, the *Brut* is based on earlier material that survives in more than one version and is, therefore, a multiple source. Taking their name from the manuscripts from which they are identified, the two most important vernacular variants of the *Brut* include *Peniarth MS 20*

and the *Red Book of Hergest*. A third and closely related
version, the *Brenhinedd y Saesson* or *Kings of the Saxons* is a
composite source the first half of which, up to and including the
year 1197, represents an independent variant that incorporates
material from English annals, but after 1198 follows almost
exactly the *Peniarth MS 20* version. (They have been edited and
translated in a series of volumes by Thomas Jones and published
by the University of Wales Press.)

That the twelfth-century redactions of the *Brut* have a
southern Welsh provenance is well attested, the scribes being
thought to hail from the cathedral church of St David's and
the monasteries of Llanbadarn Fawr and Strata Florida.
Consequently, the *Brut* has a great deal more to say about
Deheubarth and its princes than about their rival counterparts in
Gwynedd. This is particularly marked in the thirty years after the
death of Owain Gwynedd in 1170 for, as Charles Insley has
stated, 'The contrast between the last decades of the twelfth
century and the first few of the thirteenth, in terms of what we
know about Gwynedd, could not be greater.'[20] Although the
number of references to Gwynedd in the annals did improve
significantly once Llywelyn had come to dominate the political
scene (the scribes could hardly ignore him), it is noteworthy that,
at his death, this 'Great' prince merited only a six-line eulogy in
one version of the *Brut* as opposed to the two pages plus given
over to the Lord Rhys.[21]

That there was an annalistic tradition peculiar to Gwynedd is
suggested by the survival of a tract known as *O Oes Gwrtheyrn
Gertheneu* (*From the Age of Vortigern*) which consists of a series
of chronologically arranged notes recording events in north
Wales.[22] Unfortunately, neither it nor the other chronicles say
very much on the more significant events in Gwynedd's history
such as the rise to power of Llywelyn ap Iorwerth which, as A.D.
Carr rightly pointed out, is 'surely a worthy theme for the
historian of the Welsh princes.'[23] Two further chronicles of
importance are the Latin *Annales Cambriae* and *Cronica de
Wallia* (the latter covering the period from 1190 to 1266); both
are thought to be closely related to the lost Latin exemplars upon

which the versions of the *Brut* are based. Imperfectly published in 1860 by J. Williams ab Ithel (Rolls Series) a new edition of the *Annales* is currently being undertaken. The *Cronica de Wallia* on the other hand, was not published until 1946, some seven years after its discovery in Exeter Cathedral Library.[24]

Few historians would question the value of these chronicles as sources for pre-conquest Welsh history, if only because they were written by Welshmen who would have had a greater understanding and appreciation of Welsh affairs than their English or European counterparts. However, they are not without their problems for they were written and translated in the second half of the thirteenth century by monks far removed from the time they were describing and although some of the evidence they used and copied may date from an earlier time, a lost Latin archetype, we cannot be sure of the accuracy of their transcriptions or where hindsight has influenced the text. Nor are they – and this applies to other contemporary sources also – unbiased or objective, being often subject to reworking in the interests of politically dominant dynasties and institutions. Again, when different versions of the *Brut* are compared for information they can occasionally prove contradictory, though this can sometimes be a benefit by offering a different perspective.

If the rulers of Gwynedd did not benefit from frequent reference in the native *Brutiau*, they did at least attract the interest of English kings and, by implication, their clerks who were responsible for compiling royal records. Consequently, these records, particularly those dating from the thirteenth century, are rich sources for many aspects of Welsh history including the ruling princes. Among the more useful records are the calendars published for the History and Law Series, *Calendar of Ancient Correspondence concerning Wales* and *Littere Wallie* edited by J.G. Edwards. The native rulers were no less productive, albeit on a much smaller scale, in issuing charters, letters and other acts, the sum total of which have been published in a monumental work entitled *The Acts of Welsh Rulers 1120-1283*. Expertly edited by Huw Pryce, the work succeeds in making more accessible a key body of source material for the

study of medieval Wales and may be considered a perfect
companion to J.E. Lloyd's *History of Wales*. In all some sixty-
two charters, letters and agreements survive from the reign of
Llywelyn, placing him second only to his grandson, Llywelyn ap
Gruffudd, for whom well over a hundred such documents are
extant.

A number of princes attained sufficient eminence, or infamy,
to attract the attention of English and continental chroniclers.
Among the more significant of the late twelfth- and thirteenth-
century chroniclers were Roger of Howden (d.*c*.1201), Ralph of
Diceto (d.*c*.1203), Ralph of Coggeshall (fl.1210), Roger of
Wendover (d.1236) and, especially, Matthew Paris (d.1259) and
his *Chronica Maiora*. Their usefulness lies in the fact that they
were well-informed contemporaries with a sound knowledge of
much of what they wrote while some were closely connected
with, or employed by, the English royal court. Matthew Paris,
for example, makes an important reference to Llywelyn ap
Iorwerth's stroke in 1237, an event that apparently escaped the
pens, if not the notice, of the native chroniclers. The odd nugget
of valuable information notwithstanding, Paris and his
contemporaries were foreigners with little, or at best peripheral,
knowledge of Welsh affairs and much of the information they
supply on Wales is often incidental and occasionally distorted.
The same cautionary note must be applied to those few
anonymously written monastic annals and chronicles of the reigns
of various English monarchs that make reference to Wales and its
princes. On the other hand, monastic cartularies are a rich and
sober source of information on church property and related
matters that might involve the princes often in some conveyance,
dispute or damage. Taken in conjunction with the evidence
culled from the native chroniclers, these various sources do at
least provide some rounding of the picture of the native rulers of
Wales.

The Twelfth-Century Renaissance witnessed the beginning
of one of the great periods of vernacular, or non-Latin, poetry,
and in Wales therefore the works of the court poets or
Gogynfeirdd (The Poets of the Princes) cannot be ignored for,

archaism and hyperbole apart, if used with caution, they provide much historical information not forgetting a valuable social and political perspective. In a fitting tribute to their work, the University of Wales Centre for Advanced Welsh and Celtic Studies at Aberystwyth is in the process of editing the works of the Gogynfeirdd. Pride of place in the Welsh-language *Cyfres Beirdd* series must surely go to *Llywarch ap Llywelyn, 'Prydydd y Moch'*, who became the chief court poet to Llywelyn ap Iorwerth. Close on forty court poets have been identified, of whom at least eight addressed their poetry to Llywelyn. As the dates of their composition suggest – *c.*1250-1330 – the texts of the poems survive only in later copies so that they must be approached with a degree of circumspection though, in the majority of cases, it can be argued that they were faithfully reproduced from the originals. The most useful guide in English to their works, though sadly lacking an index, is J.E. Caerwyn Williams, *The Poets of the Welsh Princes.*

Of equal if not greater importance were the literary compositions of writers who were not content just to record events in annalistic form but were keen to describe their experiences, travels and opinions, especially of those they knew and others they had met. One such writer – Gerald of Wales – towers above his contemporaries and his writings are perhaps among the most frequently used and potentially the most valuable sources for the history of twelfth- and early thirteenth-century Wales. The significance of his voluminous works lies in the fact that they originated in the mind, and emanated from the pen, of a contemporary who knew well the people and country he was describing (see above). As the son of William de Barri, an Anglo-Norman lord of Manorbier, and Angharad, the grand-daughter of Rhys ap Tewdwr (d.1093), king of Deheubarth, Gerald was the product of the twelfth-century March who lived his life torn between two worlds never fully reconciling himself to either, though in his heart one might suspect, he was more Anglo-Norman than Welsh. Thus, being of mixed race but noble parentage, holding a respected position in the church and by virtue of his contacts with the courts of Welsh rulers and English kings alike, Gerald was well placed to comment on the political, social and religious scene.

Unfortunately, Llywelyn ap Iorwerth did not share in the good fortune that attended his great-grandfather, Gruffudd ap Cynan of Gwynedd, of whom a biography was written, a Welsh translation of a Latin original, some thirty years after his death. Approved if not commissioned by his son and successor, Owain Gwynedd, the *Historia Gruffud vab Kenan* is the only near-contemporary biography to be written of a Welsh prince, or at least the only one to have survived. There is some evidence dating from the seventeenth century to suggest that biographies were composed for the Gwynedd dynasts Llywelyn ap Iorwerth and his son Dafydd. The manuscript(s) were known to the eminent antiquaries Edward Lhuyd and Robert Vaughan of Hengwrt, and were thought to be preserved in St Bennet's (now Corpus Christi) College, Cambridge, but no trace of them survives.[25] Interestingly, Nicholas Robinson, bishop of Bangor between 1566 and 1585, and a graduate of Queen's College, Cambridge, where he spent the best part of twenty years, makes reference to 'the lives of a troublesome prince or two'.

While we value the work of the antiquarian collectors of old manuscripts we must not be too hasty in condemning as fiction the treatises of these same sixteenth- and seventeenth-century antiquaries. Certainly, if used with caution, Humphrey Llwyd's *Cronica Walliae* and Sir John Wynn's *History of the Gwydir Family* can add significant details to our knowledge of the period. Although based largely on versions of the *Brut*, English chronicles and Gerald of Wales, it is possible that Llwyd and, to a lesser extent, Wynn may have had to hand manuscripts now lost to us. Loss, destruction, accident and sheer bad luck together with the good intentions of the unwitting and the unwary have conspired to reduce much of our written history to priceless fragments. Nevertheless, from the evidence that does survive historians can, at the very least, begin to reconstruct the lives and careers of men like Llywelyn who played such a dominant role in the history of medieval Wales.

Notes

[1] J. Beverley Smith's magisterial book on the life and career of Llywelyn ap Gruffudd has come closest to that elusive biography of a Welsh prince. See Smith, J.B., *Llywelyn ap Gruffudd Prince of Wales* (Cardiff, 1998),

[2] The carved stone head found at Deganwy Castle is thought by some to represent the face of its builder, Llywelyn ap Iorwerth. In his illustrated chronicle Matthew Paris depicts Llywelyn on his death-bed attended by his sons Dafydd and Gruffudd.

[3] Thorpe, L. (ed.)., *The Journey through Wales, and The Description of Wales by Gerald of Wales* (Harmondsworth, 1978), 220.

[4] *Ibid.*, 221.

[5] Pryce, Huw, 'In search of a medieval society: Deheubarth in the writings of Gerald of Wales', *Welsh History Review*, 13 (1987), 281.

[6] *Ibid.*, 266.

[7] Stephenson, D., *The Governance of Gwynedd* (Cardiff, 1984), xv.

[8] *The Journey and Description*, 194.

[9] *Ibid.*, 194.

[10] *Ibid.*, 182.

[11] Jones, A.R. & Tydeman, W., *A Pedestrian Tour through North Wales in a Series of Letters by J. Hucks* (Cardiff, 1979), 47.

[12] *The Journey and Description*, 187.

[13] *Ibid.*, 187.

[14] *Ibid.*, 196.

[15] *Ibid.*, 196.

[16] Stephenson, *op.cit.*, xvi.

[17] Richter, M., 'The Political and Institutional background to National Consciousness in Medieval Wales', in Moody, T.W. (ed.), *Nationality and the Pursuit of National Independence* (Belfast, 1978), 38.

[18] Evans, D. Simon, *A Mediaeval Prince of Wales: The Life of Gruffudd ap Cynan* (Llanerch, 1990), 81, 82.

[19] Insley, Charles, 'The wilderness years of Llywelyn the Great', in Prestwich, Michael; Britnell, Richard Hugh; Frame, Robin (ed.), *Thirteenth-Century England IX: Proceedings of the Durham Conference, 2001* (Woodbridge, 2003), 163.

[20] *Ibid.*, 163.

[21] Jones, Thomas (ed.), *Brut y Tywysogyon, or, Chronicle of the Princes: Peniarth MS 20 version* (Cardiff, 1952), 76-8, 105.

[22] See Rhys, J. & Gwenogvryn Evans, J. (eds.), *The Text of the Bruts from the Red Book of Hergest* (Oxford, 1890).

[23] Carr, A.D., *Medieval Wales* (London, 1995), 6.

[24] The value of each of these chronicles together with a discussion of their textual problems is provided by Thomas Jones in 'Cronica de Wallia and other documents from Exeter Cathedral Library MS 3154', *BBCS*, 12 (1946-8), 17-44 and by Kathleen Hughes in 'The Welsh Latin Chronicles: Annales Cambriae and related texts', *Proceedings of the British Academy*, 59 (1973), 233-58.

[25] Gunther, R.T., *Early Science in Oxford 14: Life and Letters of Edward Lhwyd* (Oxford, 1945), 371.

Table 1 The dynasty of Gwynedd

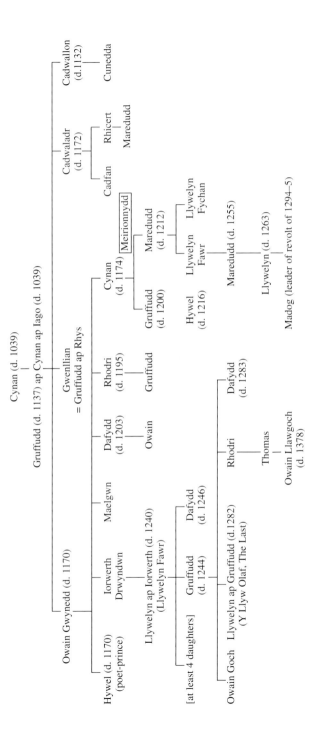

II

Dynastic Strife:
The Wilderness Years of Llywelyn ap Iorwerth,
c.1173–88

> Owain ap Gruffudd ap Cynan, prince of Gwynedd, the man who was of great goodness and very great nobility and wisdom, the bulwark of all Wales, after innumerable victories, and unconquered from his youth, without ever having refused anyone that for which he asked, died.[1]

> [*Brut y Tywysogyon*, 1170]

To the native chronicler, Owain Gwynedd was, clearly, a man worthy of the highest praise but to Gerald of Wales he was an excommunicant guilty of entering into an incestuous marriage. Nevertheless, even Gerald was forced to admit that, for over thirty years, Owain had governed Gwynedd with 'equity, prudence and princely moderation'.[2] Owain's death created a void that could not easily be filled and although he was able to control his quarrelsome sons during his lifetime, he failed to ensure a smooth succession. Within months of his death, war had broken out as the family set itself the brutal and bloody task of choosing a successor. There followed almost three decades of struggle for the control of Gwynedd among Owain's sons and grandsons, a dynastic conflict that was finally resolved with the ascendancy of Llywelyn ap Iorwerth.

FRATRICIDE AND THE SUCCESSION TO OWAIN GWYNEDD

No sooner had Owain Gwynedd been laid to rest in the cathedral church at Bangor, sometime in October or November 1170, than his sons fell out over the succession. Before the year was out, Owain's eldest son and likely heir, the poet-prince, Hywel ab Owain, was killed by his half-brothers Dafydd and Rhodri at the battle of Pentraeth in Anglesey. Clearly rulership was an obligation not for the faint-hearted since an heir-designate needed more than simply a sound pedigree, status and seniority to succeed; strength of character, martial courage, ruthless politicking and not a little luck were all equally essential. Gerald of Wales had no doubt as to the cause of this apparent ruthless 'disregard of brotherly ties':[3]

> [A] serious cause of dissension is the habit of the Welsh princes of entrusting the education of each of their sons to a different nobleman living in their territory. If the prince happens to die, each nobleman plots and plans to enforce the succession of his own foster-brother and to make sure that he is preferred to the other brothers. It follows that you will find that friendships are much warmer between foster-brothers than they are between true brothers.[4]

Apart from this revealing insight into the upbringing of royal children we know little of the domestic side of life in the households of the princes. Not surprisingly, perhaps, given Gerald's authority, we learn that Hywel was accompanied in battle by six of his foster-brothers, the sons of Cydifor Wyddel (the Irishman), all of whom bar one, the warrior-poet Peryf ap Cedifor, perished alongside their royal 'sibling'. The poet's wrath is firmly directed at the one brother whom he holds responsible for this outrage:

> Woe to you, cruel Dafydd,
> To stab tall Hywel, hawk of war![5]

Disputed succession and territorial fragmentation was an unfortunate fact of Welsh political life during the twelfth and thirteenth centuries. The Welsh law of partible inheritance ensured that if there were many sons or heirs the property would be shared equally between them. The danger inherent in operating such a system was obvious to Gerald: 'Quarrels and lawsuits result, murders and arson, not to mention frequent fratricides.'[6] Socially these laws had much to commend them but politically they spelt disaster. The ownership of land implies some form of power and those to whom was entrusted the power to own land were either royal or noble in status. Their land holding invariably involved lordship since theirs was a land in which others lived and over whom they exercised their authority. Therefore, these were more than simply units of land, but units of political power presided over by rulers who had at their disposal military as well as economic resources commensurate with their status. In such circumstances, partible inheritance had the potential to destroy not only the integrity of existing units of land, and the accumulation of additional landed units, but also the political power that went with them.

However, in a society where the principle of division seemed paramount, there remained at least one essential element that was indivisible: the rulership. Irrespective of whether the ruler was called a king or prince, the evolution of royal nomenclature had blurred somewhat the distinction between titles; the power vested in the ruler to govern the kingdom and lead the people in war remained the same. Therefore, the land might be divided and the power might be dissipated but the title and authority of the rulership, the dignity of which had a special legal status, devolved undivided to those who succeeded by hereditary right. Of course, this does not mean that royal successions went unchallenged; Hywel's death at the hands of his brothers is evidence of that, for although succession by hereditary right need only to be based on royal blood, neither law nor custom offered much in the way of precision in specifying who was or who was not eligible. In so far as the ruling elite derived their status from their kindred, the dynasty, rather than any individual, was heir, in which case sons, nephews and even cousins might be eligible to succeed. Only by publicly designating an heir or successor during his lifetime could a ruler like Owain Gwynedd hope to pass on intact his inheritance in territory and authority. That he may have failed to do so – historians can only hint at Hywel's status as heir-designate – might explain why civil war broke out so soon after Owain's death.

This is not to suggest that Owain Gwynedd would have left destitute his remaining sons and near kinsmen, since it was the custom for each to be provided with an estate located within the bounds of the kingdom. It has been suggested that Dafydd's share of the patrimony included half of the land east of the river Conwy, known as Gwynedd Is Conwy or the Perfeddwlad, centred on the lordships or cantrefi of Tegeingl and Dyffryn Clwyd. In the land west of the Conwy, known as Gwynedd Uwch Conwy, Rhodri held sway in the cantref of Llŷn whilst his half-brothers, Maelgwn and Cynan, were apportioned Anglesey and Meirionnydd respectively.[7] The least known of the sons of Owain Gwynedd, Iorwerth Drwyndwn (Flat or broken-nosed), is believed to have been given the commote of Nantconwy. What Cadwaladr, Owain Gwynedd's younger brother, received as his share is not known but his death in 1172 removed him from the competition.

What re-arrangements for partition were made after the death of Hywel is not known but suffice it to say that peace did not reign long in Gwynedd, for no sooner had Dafydd and Rhodri dispatched their half-brother than they turned on each other. During 1173-4, Dafydd sought to make himself sole ruler of Gwynedd by dispossessing and imprisoning his younger brother Rhodri and by forcing his half-brother Maelgwn into exile in Ireland. Cynan died before he too, presumably, could be ousted but he was succeeded by his sons, Gruffudd and Maredudd, the latter of whom had greeted Gerald of Wales on his first setting foot in Gwynedd. Fratricidal strife notwithstanding, Dafydd found time and men to support the English king, Henry II, who was similarly engaged in a civil war after his sons turned against him. This was a clever move on Dafydd's part for in supporting the ultimately successful king, he gained Henry's backing in his quest for the rulership of Gwynedd. In a further, hitherto unprecedented move, the king also agreed, in the summer of 1174, to give his illegitimate half-sister, Emma of Anjou, in marriage to Dafydd. This was a significant dynastic alliance and one that Dafydd hoped might help secure him the rulership of Gwynedd. The chronicler of the *Brut* certainly thought so for, as he wrote, the prince 'married the king's sister because he thought that he could hold his territory in peace thereby.'[8]

Dafydd was to be disappointed: there is no evidence of significant English military support and, within a year of his marriage, Rhodri had escaped from prison, Maelgwn had returned from exile and war was resumed. Dafydd was driven out of all the land west of the river Conwy, while the sons of Cynan may have entered the fray to secure Meirionnydd as their share of the spoils. They were certainly in possession of Meirionnydd by 1177-8 when they successfully resisted an attempt by the Lord Rhys, prince of Deheubarth, to annex the lordship. By that time also some sort of deal seems to have been struck between Dafydd and Rhodri in which Gwynedd was partitioned: Rhodri gained control of Gwynedd Uwch Conwy including Anglesey and its court of Aberffraw, while Dafydd secured the whole of Gwynedd Is Conwy along with, arguably, the rulership of the kingdom. The fact that Dafydd alone of the royal house of Gwynedd attended King Henry II at the Council of Oxford in 1177 suggests that he, rather than Rhodri or Maelgwn (who was probably dead by this time), was ruler of the kingdom. Again, of all the Welsh princes who attended the Oxford Council, Dafydd and the Lord Rhys alone were required to do homage to the king which A.D. Carr has taken as a sign that there may have been a 'polarization of native political authority in Wales with Dafydd and Rhys being recognized as the dominant rulers in the north and in the south.'[9]

However, Charles Insley has countered by suggesting 'that it was not as simple as that' inasmuch as Dafydd's presence at Oxford 'may indicate his weakness as much as his strength', because he might have been 'seeking English legitimation of his position in Gwynedd.'[10] It is interesting to note that in the late sixteenth-century *History of the Gwydir Family,* the author, Sir John Wynn, states that Dafydd only maintained Rhuddlan castle with the aid of 'a garrison of English'.[11] As far as the poet Llywarch ap Llywelyn is concerned, whoever held Aberffraw was 'inherent chief ruler' not just of Gwynedd but of Wales also.[12] Although this might be taken as the expected boast of a northern court poet, it is significant that, in the context of north Wales alone, he persists in celebrating the authority of Aberffraw and that for him, and presumably his knowing audience, whoever is described as 'lord of Aberffraw' holds the rulership of the kingdom. Thus does the poet address as lord of Aberffraw firstly Dafydd (*c.*1172-5) followed by Rhodri (*c.*1175-94). This would suggest that Rhodri and not Dafydd held the rulership of Gwynedd when the latter was summoned to attend the king at Oxford.

Whatever the truth of the matter, Rhodri and Dafydd continued to fight each other spasmodically between the late 1170s and the mid-1190s. Although neither was strong enough to completely dominate let alone eliminate the other, if the poet Llywarch ap Llywelyn is to be believed, the pendulum of power was most definitely swinging Rhodri's way during the 1180s. Indeed, unlike his brother who looked outward and sought English help for his cause, Rhodri turned inward and southward for support by marrying the daughter of the most powerful Welshman of his day, the Lord Rhys of Deheubarth. According to Gerald of Wales, Rhodri 'had taken this woman to gain the support of Rhys against his own brothers' sons, whom he had disinherited.'[13] However, like his brother Dafydd, Rhodri too 'met with disappointment instead of the support on which he had counted.'[14]

It is a matter of regret that Gerald decided to 'pass in silence what was done by Owain's sons in our own days, when he himself was dead or dying.'[15] Fortunately, he did mention that although Owain Gwynedd 'had many sons' only one, he believed, was legitimate:

> This was Iorwerth Drwyndwn, which is the Welsh for flat-nosed. He in his turn had a legitimate son called Llywelyn.[16]

This is interesting because it is almost certainly incorrect: Maelgwn is also thought to have been the son of Owain

Gwynedd by his first wife Gwladus, the daughter of Llywarch ap Trahaearn of Arwystli, but it reflects well the influence of hindsight on the author. Gerald took the opportunity to revise his work so that at the time of the re-writing of his *Journey through Wales* (between the first version in 1191 and third in *c*.1214) Llywelyn had established himself as the ruler of Gwynedd. Ever one to indulge his fondness for moral strictures, Gerald would have been keen to point out that unlike Owain Gwynedd's first wife, his second, Cristin, was closely related to him. Consequently, Iorwerth's half-brothers, Dafydd and Rhodri, the sons of Cristin, were 'born in incest' so that their defeat at the hands of their nephew Llywelyn, who could 'trust in the vengeance of God', demonstrates 'how much those who commit adultery and incest are displeasing in the eyes of God.'[17] Therefore, Llywelyn's eventual triumph was, in the mind of Gerald, a divine vindication of legitimacy. What Gerald neglected to say was that Llywelyn was himself a product of an adulterous marriage since his father Iorwerth had taken to wife his cousin, Marared of Powys!

IORWERTH DRWYNDWN AB OWAIN GWYNEDD

One brother only appears not to have taken part in the dynastic strife that engulfed the family after the death of Owain Gwynedd, namely, Iorwerth Drwyndwn. Iorwerth made no impact on the historical record, so that much of what we know of him comes to us by way of the poet rather than of the chronicler. The poet in question was Seisyll Bryffwrch, a professional bard who had performed in the courts of Deheubarth and Powys before making his way to Gwynedd where he sang elegiac odes on the death of Owain Gwynedd and of Iorwerth. Indeed, Seisyll Bryffwrch may not have been the only poet to sing Iorwerth's praises, since there is evidence to suggest that Elidir Sais may also have addressed poetry to Llywelyn's father. If this is so, then Iorwerth was clearly not as inconsequential as the historical record makes out.

News has come to me, it is painful to remember it,
Immense news, wondrously sad,
News that is too much, too hard to share,
Very painful news is the death of Owain's great son,
Recently in the south and east,
It is too much, it is grief for Britain,
All the bards are empty-handed after the death of a friend,
And many memories offer themselves to them.
After poets weaken, it is not good to bear this news,
From here to Rome,
Because the skilful leader is dead,
Sadder news, horrendous is their walk over hills;
To Maig there is no resurrection,
It will be no good to the lands of Christendom,
[because] the tight and cold shroud of earth and stones
of Llandutglyd is around [one who was] a raiser of praise,
The Lord of Dygen, a kindly and wonderful
Lord of Arfon, Iorwerth son of Owain.[18]

Unfortunately, it is not possible to date accurately the elegy but the consensus of opinion is that Iorwerth was dead by the mid-to-late 1170s.

We are led to believe that Iorwerth played no part in the power struggle either because he was facially disfigured or physically disabled. Certainly, his epithet Trwyndwn might literally refer to a nasal deformity but it may also be indicative of something much worse. For example, in his *History of the Gwydir Family*, Wynn thought that Iorwerth was 'unfit to govern by reason of the deformities of his face.'[19] The poet, Seisyll Bryffwrch, makes no mention of any such deformity or disability but that is perhaps to be expected given the eulogistic conventions that governed poetic composition at the time. According to J.E. Lloyd,

> The blemishes which excluded an heir under Welsh law were only those which incapacitated for judicial or military duties.[20]

If Iorwerth was thought unfit to perform these duties, why then was he believed capable of being, in the words of the poet, 'ruler of Arfon'? Again, it is significant that in spite of his perceived disability he was considered a worthy candidate for marriage and fit enough to beget a healthy son. If, as tradition affirms, Iorwerth was married to Marared, daughter of Madog ap Maredudd, the last and, arguably, greatest of the princes of a united Powys, then this was a good match. It was part of a dual dynastic alliance between Gwynedd and Powys for Madog ap Maredudd's son, Gruffudd Maelor, was married to Iorwerth's sister, Angharad.

It is to Gerald of Wales that we owe the reference to the epithet of Trwyndwn though he fails to explain its significance, perhaps expecting his readers to possess such understanding which is denied us through the passage of time. Was this a defect suffered from birth or had he acquired it by accident or through war? We simply do not know, but it is worth noting that Humphrey Llwyd, the sixteenth-century antiquary, suggested that though he was the 'eldest sonne borne in matrimonye'; Iorwerth's leadership credentials were 'counted unmeete for his *maime* upon the face'.[21] It was once thought that Iorwerth died

Photograph of Dolwyddelan Castle.   *(Cadw, Crown copyright)*

in exile in Powys but the poet, Seisyll Bryffwrch, makes it clear
that Llywelyn's father remained in Gwynedd and was buried in
the church at Penmachno.

LLYWELYN'S BIRTH AND EARLY LIFE

Tradition has firmly fixed the date and location of Llywelyn's
birth to the early part of 1173 in the castle of Dolwyddelan.
Situated at the heart of Snowdonia in the shadow of Moel
Siabod, the Dolwyddelan of Llywelyn's birth is unlikely to be the
one currently popular with the modern visitor. This castle was
almost certainly the work of Llywelyn and was likely built in the
early thirteenth century to replace the earlier, simpler stone
structure of his birth, the remains of which can still be seen a
little way below the partially reconstructed Dolwyddelan. Who
built this twelfth-century stone castle is not known but from
Gerald of Wales we learn that the sons and grandsons of Owain
Gwynedd were actively engaged in castle construction before his
journey of 1188. If, as tradition suggests, Iorwerth was lord of
Nantconwy, might he have been its builder? That same tradition
states that on the death of his father, Llywelyn, who was but an
infant, was taken for safety from his home at Dolwyddelan to his
mother's land of Powys, where he grew from childhood into
youth.

   Given the fate of rival siblings in previous familial encounters
in Gwynedd's bloody dynastic history, this tale of the spiriting
away of the young Llywelyn is entirely reasonable. Less than a
generation before his birth, Llywelyn's own grandfather, Owain
Gwynedd, had been responsible for the maiming, in 1152, of 'his
nephew, his brother's son', Cunedda ap Cadwallon, by depriving
him of 'his eyes and his testicles'.[22] Gerald was well aware of the
bloody consequences of family rivalry and a disputed succession:

> The most frightful disturbances occur in their territories as a
> result, people being murdered, brothers killing each other and
> even putting each other's eyes out, for as everyone knows from
> experience it is very difficult to settle disputes of this sort.[23]

Ever the wit, Gerald managed to find some grim humour in his treatise on Welsh familial relationships:

> It is also remarkable how much more people love their brothers when they are dead than they do when they are still alive. They will persecute their living brothers until they bring about their death; but when their brothers die, especially if someone else happens to have killed them, they will move heaven and earth to avenge them.[24]

Would that we knew more of Llywelyn's supposed flight to, and subsequent upbringing in, Powys. His mother Marared may have been a member of the Powysian dynasty but this did not, in itself, offer her any greater security than she might have enjoyed with her late husband's household in Gwynedd. Who would have taken her in and protected her and, more to the point, why? Her father was long dead and the land she called home had been carved up between his sons, her brothers, and his nephew, Owain Cyfeiliog. One might speculate that, of her brothers, Elise, Owain Fychan, Owain Brogyntyn, and Gruffudd Maelor, the last seems the most likely to have extended his protection to his sister and nephew. Famed for being 'the most generous of the Welsh',[25] Gruffudd Maelor, ruler of Powys Fadog, was married to Iorwerth's sister, Angharad, and their son, Madog, subsequently proved to be among the most loyal and trustworthy of Llywelyn's princely supporters. In stark contrast, Llywelyn's rough treatment of Elise – taking from him the territory of Penllyn in 1202 – would have been scant reward for his protection had the latter ever been disposed to offer it.

Of course, Powys was not the only refuge available to the infant Llywelyn even if it is the most likely. Ireland had long played host to the dispossessed and destitute Welsh princes, Llywelyn's great-grandfather, Gruffudd ap Cynan, among them having been born in Dublin. Around the time of Llywelyn's birth, his uncle, Maelgwn, had sought shelter there and may even have held land in the vicinity of Dublin. In 1218 an inquisition was held in the city to determine the extent of this property and to decide if Llywelyn, as the childless Maelgwn's nearest living relative, was entitled to claim it.[26] On the other hand, there is some evidence to suggest that Llywelyn may have had the Corbets of Caus to thank for his upbringing. In a copy of a letter preserved among the manuscripts of the Wynns of Gwydir and tentatively dated to the summer of 1212, Llywelyn refers to the monk Walter Corbet as his kinsman and close friend, and to William Corbet as his uncle. This has led to the entirely plausible suggestion that Llywelyn's widowed mother had married a member of an English Marcher family whose Shropshire lordship of Caus abutted Powys. In the opinion of Kari Maund, the fact that Llywelyn had shown himself to be adept at dealing with the Marcher lords and with English court politics 'could well be a by-product of an education in the mixed Anglo-Welsh world of the March'.[27]

The simple truth is that we do not know nor are we likely to find out where or by what means Llywelyn was protected and sustained in his early 'wilderness' years. What is certain is that as he grew to manhood, he learnt that he had rights of inheritance which he was being denied. Gerald is the first to take note of the young prince, stating that when he and Archbishop Baldwin were passing through North Wales in 1188, Llywelyn had already begun to

> attack his two uncles, Dafydd and Rhodri [who] shared between them as their inheritance the whole of Gwynedd except the land of Cynan.[28]

Although Llywelyn was older than the twelve years suggested by Gerald – he was more likely fourteen or fifteen years old – he was probably as 'destitute of lands and money' as he is described. Unlike his uncles who 'had their own wealth to draw on and the support of other rich men',[29] Llywelyn may only have had the aid of his mother's kinsfolk to rely on. Undaunted, Llywelyn set forth on his adventure to assert his claim to a share of Gwynedd, a journey that would take him nearly twenty years to fulfil.

Notes

1 *BT. Pen.*, 65.
2 *The Journey and Description*, 203.
3 *Ibid.*, 193.
4 *Ibid.*, 261.
5 Caerwyn Williams, J.E., *The Poets of the Welsh Princes* (Cardiff, 1978), 28.
6 *The Journey and Description*, 261.
7 This may post-date the death of Owain Gwynedd.
8 *BT. Pen.*, 70.
9 Carr, A.D., *NewDNB*, online edn.
10 Insley, 'The wilderness years', 165.
11 Wynn, John, Sir. *The History of the Gwydir Family, and Memoirs.*; ed. Jones. J.G. (Llandysul, 1990), 3.
12 Jarman, A.O.H & Hughes, G.R. (eds.), *A Guide to Welsh Literature* (2 vols., Swansea, 1976; repr., 1979), I, 152.
13 *The Journey and Description*, 186.
14 Gerald of Wales calls her his 'mistress'. *The Journey and Description*, 186.
15 *Ibid.*, 193.
16 *Ibid.*, 193.
17 *Ibid.*, 194.
18 Translation by Einir Jones.
19 *History of the Gwydir Family*, 3.
20 Lloyd, J.E., *A History of Wales from earliest times to the Edwardian Conquest* (2 vols., London, 1911), II, 550n.69.
21 Llwyd, Humphrey, *Cronica Walliae*, ed. Ieuan M. Williams (Cardiff, 2002), 167.
22 *BT.RBH*, 131.
23 *The Journey and Description*, 261.
24 *Ibid.*, 261.
25 *B. Saes.*, 189. *The Journey and Description*, 203.
26 Maund, K.L. (ed.), *Gruffudd ap Cynan: a collaborative biography* (Woodbridge, 1996), 27.
27 Maund, K.L., *The Welsh Kings* (Stroud, 2000), 116.
28 *The Journey and Description*, 193.
29 *Ibid.*, 194-5.

III

Struggle for Supremacy:
The Rise of Llywelyn ap Iorwerth,
*c.*1188-1201

Rhodri was prince at such time as the Archbishop preached the Cross in Anglesey, and that he had in his court Llywelyn, the son of Iorwerth or Edward, his nephew. Though he was overborn by his uncle Dafydd [and] his uncle Rhodri . . . yet God so advanced the right of the young Prince Llywelyn that in time he put down both his uncles from the princely sceptre and their posterity.[1]

[Sir John Wynn, *History of the Gwydir Family*, *c.*1580-1616]

It is hard to imagine, as Sir John Wynn evidently did, that Llywelyn would have found a place in the royal court of his uncle, Rhodri, at Aberffraw. Unless it was for the purpose of an alliance, Llywelyn's presence there would likely have been that of a prisoner; though he was Rhodri's nephew he was also his rival and, therefore, his enemy. Indeed, at that point in his fledgling career, the teenage Llywelyn would probably not have appeared too attractive an ally to an uncle who counted the Lord Rhys among his supporters. Throughout the 1180s, Rhodri's stock had been rising while that of his chief rival, Dafydd, dependent as he was on English support, was falling. It looked to all the world as if Rhodri would, once and for all, settle in his favour the succession to Owain Gwynedd but events took an unexpected turn when Llywelyn appeared on the scene. However, Llywelyn's victory over his uncles was neither as certain nor inevitable as Sir John Wynn, writing with the benefit of hindsight, would have us believe. He was not alone in challenging the right of Rhodri to govern the heartland of Gwynedd and its ancient court of Aberffraw, for his cousins, the sons of Cynan, had also rekindled their hopes of securing the rulership of the kingdom. The scene was set for a titanic battle for supremacy in Gwynedd.

FIRST STEPS TO POWER IN GWYNEDD

The steps by which Llywelyn rose to the height of his ambition and made himself the primary ruler of Gwynedd are not easy to trace. Our principal source for the history of the period, the *Brut y Tywysogyon,* makes no mention of Llywelyn until 1194 when he was twenty-one years old. The poets offer much in the way of anecdotal evidence but their craft and cryptic references pose problems of interpretation. The evidence for Llywelyn's rise to power begins with Gerald of Wales who, if his recollection of events is correct, states that the young prince began his fight for a share of the patrimony in the early months of 1188. We lose sight of Llywelyn for some six years, until 1194, when the *Brut* records his first major military campaign:

> In that year, Llywelyn ap Iorwerth and the two sons of Cynan ab Owain and Rhodri ab Owain united together against Dafydd ab Owain and they drove him to flight and took from him all his territory except three castles.[2]

This alliance was probably one born of necessity rather than entered into freely. For some years previously there had been quarrels between Rhodri and his energetic younger nephews, Gruffudd and Maredudd, the sons of Cynan. Sometime between 1190 and 1191 the latter had driven Rhodri out of Anglesey, whereupon he turned for help to Rognvald, the recently crowned king of Man and the Isles (1188-1226). As a pledge of alliance, Rhodri agreed to marry, in 1192, Rognvald's daughter and, in the following year with the aid of a substantial levy of Manx troops and ships, he expelled his nephews from Anglesey.[3] We are never told what had happened to Rhodri's first wife, the daughter of the Lord Rhys, but if Gerald's gossip is to be believed, they were never married but lived together in sin, she as his mistress. In the event, the Manx alliance proved shortlived for as J.E. Lloyd noted, 'before the year was out their work had been undone, and the sons of Cynan had again ejected Rhodri.'[4] Clearly, Rhodri and his nephews made for uneasy bedfellows but the glue that held them together may have been the young Llywelyn who, as the *Brut* makes clear, was the driving force behind the victory in what the poet Llywarch ap Llywelyn called the battle of Aberconwy.[5]

It is to the poets that historians must reluctantly turn to trace Llywelyn's next move. In poems bereft of chronology, Cynddelw Brydydd Mawr and Llywarch ap Llywelyn hail Llywelyn's victories in two hard-fought battles on Anglesey: one on the Menai and the other inland at Coedanau. Llywelyn's enemies are nowhere described clearly but it has been suggested that the O Oes *Gwrtheyrn Gertheneuand* refers to a battle at Coedanau in 1194; his foe was his erstwhile ally Rhodri. Whatever the truth of the matter, the aged Rhodri did not long survive his defeat, for he died in 1195. It is possible but not certain that on Rhodri's death his patrimony was divided between his nephews Gruffudd and Maredudd. In his ode addressed to Gruffudd ap Cynan, Llywarch ap Llywelyn describes him as lord of Cemais and lord of Deganwy which implies his control over Anglesey and Gwynedd Uwch Conwy. His younger brother Maredudd presumably held Meirionnydd and a portion of Llŷn. At this stage of his career, Llywelyn appears to have taken most of Gwynedd Is Conwy as his share of the spoils though he had his uncle Dafydd as a disgruntled near neighbour, perhaps in Tegeingl, which fringed the border with England near Chester. For two or three years peace settled on Gwynedd but events were to show that this was but a prelude to a sustained onslaught that would see Llywelyn eliminate his rivals and claim the rulership of Gwynedd. No longer content to claim a share of the patrimony, Llywelyn had evidently set his sights on having the ultimate prize, the rulership of the whole kingdom.

THE WARRIOR PRINCE

Llywelyn's early appearance on the stage of history was evidently a memorable, if bloody, one. The poets wax lyrical about his prowess in battle, his resourcefulness and, in spite of his youth, his courage. For them he was, first and foremost, a warrior to be found in the midst of battle leading his men by heroic example. In a society where the warrior elite and the culture of war were held in high regard, it is perhaps not surprising to find Llywelyn praised so highly for his military leadership and personal prowess in arms. If the poet Llywarch sang in awe of 'the bold beloved of fortune – the terrible Llywelyn', so too did his fellow bard Cynddelw: 'Many were the foes of my lord, but there fell of them in the fight seven times the number of stars in the heavens'.[6]

True to the eulogistic tradition of contemporary native prose and poetry, chroniclers and poets magnified their patrons' personal contribution to the success of battles. Nevertheless, it must be remembered that Llywelyn stood at the apex of an aristocratic class whose shared culture was suffused with the values of a warrior elite. They were men for whom the call to arms and the blood and fury of battle were a way of life inculcated almost from birth. From an early age they were trained to master the skills of the sword, the bow and the lance, instructed in the principles of good horsemanship and taught the virtues of killing with their own hand their enemies in close combat. They were fed a diet of war stories, war poems and war songs, and, as befitted a heroic society, they imbibed the ethics of honourable war. It is an image of the Welsh as a war-hungry people that impressed itself on Gerald of Wales who states that 'In peace they dream of war and prepare themselves for battle . . . their only preoccupation is military training'; indeed 'they esteem it a disgrace to die in bed, but an honour to be killed in battle.'[7] His opinion is shared by Walter Map who speaks of 'my compatriots the Welsh' as 'warlike and skilled in arms' but whose chief glory was in 'plunder and theft', and that it was 'a reproach to a son that his father should have died without a wound.'[8]

Having made his name in the battles of Aberconwy, Menai and Coedanau, Llywelyn was once more put to the test. In 1197 war broke out between Llywelyn and his uncle Dafydd. Who or what caused this conflict to erupt is not known but, if Humphrey Llwyd's *Cronica Walliae* can be relied on, then Dafydd seems to have been its chief instigator.

> There was a great warre in Northwales, for David sonne to Owen, late prince, came with a great army, as well as Englishmen as Welshmen, thinkinge to recover the lande againe. But Lhewelyn his nevew, then in possession and right enheritor, came boldlye and mete him and gave him battaill and, puttinge his people to flight, toke him prisoner.[9]

Unless this was a plan of his own making, Dafydd may have been encouraged to attack his nephew by his English allies who were becoming increasingly concerned with Welsh affairs. In a letter to his chief justiciar, Hubert Walter, in April 1196, Richard I made plain his fear for the safety of the Welsh frontier particularly in respect of the danger posed by a resurgent Lord Rhys in the south and a rampaging Gwenwynwyn of Powys in the north. In calling for more troops to aid his campaign in France, Richard insisted that 'the barons of the March of Wales' should remain in their frontier lordships.[10] Early in 1197, Hubert Walter was sufficiently alarmed by Gwenwynwyn's growing power that he led a military expedition against him. Curiously, the *Brut* suggests that Hubert Walter's expedition to, and siege of, Gwenwynwyn's castle at Welshpool included the 'princes of Gwynedd'. Dafydd may have participated but it is difficult to imagine either Llywelyn or his cousins, the sons of Cynan, taking part.

Dafydd was likely a willing pawn in a wider English strategy to contain and distract the Welsh by setting them against each other. If this was the aim then it failed miserably for Dafydd was defeated, captured and imprisoned by Llywelyn. Not only had Llywelyn's reputation been greatly enhanced by the crushing victory but so had his power since he was now ruler of the whole of Gwynedd Is Conwy. Dafydd's imprisonment lasted less than a year for in January 1198, Walter came to the Welsh frontier to arrange, and no doubt pay for, his release. Having been 'banished from Wales' by Llywelyn, Dafydd retreated to his English manors at Ellesmere and Halesowen, both of which had been granted to him by Henry II, and there he lived with his wife, 'the royal Emma', and their son Owain until his death in 1203.

FINAL STEPS TO POWER IN GWYNEDD

In the opinion of J.E. Lloyd, 'Llywelyn was now fairly started upon his long and triumphant career'.[11] As evidence of this he cited his participation in Gwenwynwyn's great enterprise to 'restore to the Welsh', in the words of the *Brut*, 'their ancient dignity and their ancient proprietary rights and their bounds'.[12] Having secured the agreement of 'all the princes of Wales', Gwenwynwyn 'gathered a mighty host and [in August 1198] went to lay siege to Painscastle'.[13] Unfortunately for the ambitious prince of Powys, who aspired to the position of national leader of the Welsh recently vacated by the Lord Rhys who had died the year before, the expedition to Painscastle ended in disaster. Llywelyn had learnt a valuable lesson and he would never again lend command of his troops to another or participate in an expedition of which he was not leader. As for being 'fairly started upon his long and triumphant career', the truth is that he was still just a 'bit-part player' in Welsh affairs. Although Llywelyn's career was in the ascendant, he continued to live in the shadow of his cousin, Gruffudd ap Cynan, who, as the possessor of Aberffraw, could justifiably claim to be the primary prince of Gwynedd. Indeed, to the compiler of at least one version of the *Brut*, Gruffudd was by far the most powerful and greatest of the princes of Gwynedd: 'the man who was known by all in the island of Britain because of the abundance of his gifts and his gentleness and his goodness'.[14] The poet, Llywarch ap Llywelyn, agrees for in addressing Gruffudd as 'lord of Cemais' and 'lord of Deganwy' he was making clear his patron's overlordship of Gwynedd.

It is not until 1199 that Llywelyn sets about challenging his cousin Gruffudd for control of Gwynedd. The means by which he ousted Gruffudd are never made clear but it presumably included a battle or two. Llywarch ap Llywelyn appears to come to the rescue of historians when he refers to two battles fought by Llywelyn in the east, in Bro Alun, somewhere near Mold, and in the west in Arfon. If, as the poet suggests, they were fought on the same day then Llywelyn was intent on, or was forced into, fighting both his cousins and the English. Although Llywarch is keen to credit Llywelyn with victories in both battles, the fact that his patron was described by a fellow poet, Cynddelw, as the 'terror and torment of England' suggests that the prince may have personally directed his energies towards Mold. However, the poet's recollection of the battle near Mold may be suspect for although a battle was almost certainly fought there, in January 1199, corroborating references in contemporary chronicles, one compiled in England and the other in Wales, it may not have been the crushing victory Llywarch would have us believe. According to the Chester-based Chronicle of St Werburg:

> Many nobles of all north Wales were slain, and Llywelyn's men in particular were killed or scattered to a man, and Mold castle was besieged and captured from Llywelyn on the day of the Lord's Epiphany (6 January).[15]

Even taking into account the usual mix of truth, hyperbole and propaganda, the references are ambiguous as to exactly what happened at the battle near Mold. According to Cynddelw, the river 'Alun ran red' with the blood of Llywelyn's enemies but we must be prepared to accept that a fair proportion of that blood was shed by Welsh casualties. If Llywelyn suffered a defeat at Mold (some historians dispute this preferring to correct what they believe to be a corrupt, error-laden later copy of the original manuscript) it did not hinder his progress or check his ambition. Indeed, the fact that the castle had to be taken *from* Llywelyn lends credence to J.E. Lloyd's assertion, and that of the poets, that the prince had led a 'victorious assault upon the border fortress of Mold at the beginning of 1199.'[16]

As the struggle between Llywelyn and Gruffudd intensified,

there entered a new player on the political stage: King John. Succeeding Richard as king in May 1199, John was readier than his brother had been to intervene in Wales. As a consequence of his holding the lordship of Glamorgan since 1189, it has often been said that John was better acquainted with Wales than any of his predecessors. He certainly had useful experience to guide him and he brought a new focus and sharpness to Welsh affairs. His dealings with the Welsh princes were marked by a greater precision than before, but whether we can credit him, as J.E. Lloyd does, with having 'a settled and consistent policy' is debatable. John was an opportunist who twisted and turned his policies as occasion demanded but there is no compelling reason to doubt J.E. Lloyd's belief that in Wales the king's aim was to divide and to disintegrate, to checkmate the designs of the more formidable chiefs by favouring their rivals. Thus the land might be torn by the strife of opposing and not ill-balanced parties.[17]

This policy is evident almost from the time John took up the reins of power. Scarcely four months into his reign, John issued a charter, dated 28 September 1199, extending the Crown's protection to Llywelyn, confirming him in all his lands including any that he might win from his enemies. Less than two months later, on 3 December, the new king issued similar charters to Llywelyn's rival Gruffudd, and, on the following day, to Gwenwynwyn ab Owain of southern Powys. In some respects, these charters may be seen as licences to make war and fit in well with J.E. Lloyd's, admittedly 'Cambro-centric', description of John's policy of ensuring that Wales, and Gwynedd in particular, remained divided and unstable .[18]

Unfortunately, the charters do not identify either Llywelyn's or Gruffudd's landholdings; had they done so it might have gone some way to indicating who was winning the struggle for power in Gwynedd. John's charter to Llywelyn was once held to be proof positive that he was not only winning the war against his cousin Gruffudd but that he had, in fact, already won. As further proof of Llywelyn's ascendancy, a letter from Pope Innocent III to Llywelyn issued in November 1199, in which the pontiff referred to the Welshman as *princeps Norwallie* (prince of North

Wales), suggested that he and not Gruffudd was master of
Gwynedd. John's subsequent charter to Gruffudd was regarded as
a means to bolster that prince's failing fortunes.

However, this interpretation has recently been challenged by
Charles Insley who suggests that the protection offered by John
may not represent 'English acknowledgement of the extent of
Llywelyn's power but an attempt by Llywelyn to bring an extra
lever to bear in his struggle with his cousins: that of English royal
support.'[19] In fact, Llywelyn may have been following in the
footsteps of his uncles, for in seeking English support, he was
reviving the policy of Dafydd, and in petitioning the Pope to be
allowed to marry the daughter of Rognvald, King of Man, he
was restoring the familial bond established by Rhodri. Of course,
these attempts to secure external alliances may indicate
Llywelyn's weakness rather than his strength. They did little,
ultimately, to help either Dafydd or Rhodri and neither did they
do much to support Llywelyn who was left to win his war
without the aid of the English or the Manx.

The struggle between Llywelyn and Gruffudd was over by
1200 when the latter died at the abbey of Aberconwy 'after
having assumed the habit of the order'.[20] The poet, Llywarch ap
Llywelyn, suggests that Gruffudd was defeated, captured and
forcibly tonsured by Llywelyn but it is now widely thought that
he voluntarily entered the monastery, which he helped establish,
to prepare for a natural death. Whether by design or good
fortune, Llywelyn found himself on the cusp of ultimate power,
he was now just a short step from realising his ambition and all
that stood between him and the supremacy he had worked so
hard to achieve was Gruffudd's younger brother, Maredudd.
With his brother gone, Maredudd had the opportunity to shine
and seek for himself the supremacy of Gwynedd, but he was
found to be sadly wanting in ambition and may have succumbed
to Llywelyn almost without a fight.

The fact that in 1201 Llywelyn was forced to deprive
Maredudd of Llŷn and Eifionydd and, in the words of the *Brut*,
expel him 'because of his treachery', suggests that they may have
come to some form of accommodation but that this had been

betrayed. Certainly, Gerald of Wales hints that due to 'his own magnanimity and on the advice of his good counsellors', Llywelyn was prepared to forgive and forget past quarrels with those of his extended family who were willing to accept his overlordship.[21] However, if Llywelyn did this because, as Gerald naively claims, he 'pitied them still and felt some family responsibility for them', it failed miserably in the case of Maredudd who refused to accept his diminished 'client' status. On the other hand, others, like Hywel, son of his former chief rival Gruffudd, were willing to serve Llywelyn. Indeed, Llywelyn had Hywel to thank for finally putting paid to Maredudd who, having fled to Meirionnydd, was forcibly ejected by his nephew.

Not everyone hailed Llywelyn's triumph. The poet Elidir Sais protested in song at the prince's wilful flouting of the Welsh laws of inheritance and he called upon him to restore the lands to those he had dispossessed. Elidir was particularly incensed at Llywelyn's treatment of his uncle Dafydd whose enforced exile in England was considered 'to be a tyranny second only to the capture of the Holy Sepulchre by Saladin'.[22] Elidir's reward for his criticism was exile, a fate that would befall all those who dared stand against Llywelyn; he later underlined his triumph by arrogating to himself the title *tocius norwallie princeps*' or prince of the whole of North Wales. All that remained was to gain the approval and, if possible, the support of the king of England. In July 1201, this duly arrived in the shape of a peace accord negotiated and sealed beween King John and Prince Llywelyn. This 'treaty' represents the 'earliest surviving written agreement between an English monarch and a Welsh ruler',[23] and was the basis on which Llywelyn began to extend his wider hegemony beyond the bounds of his newly won principality of Gwynedd.

Notes

1 *History of the Gwydir Family*, 3-4.
2 *BT.Pen.*, 75.
3 Charles Insley is not sure who they were. 'The wilderness years', 166.
4 Lloyd, *HW*, II, 588.
5 There remains some confusion over Rhodri's role in the battle and it has been suggested that he may have fought on Dafydd's side.
6 Quoted in Lloyd, *HW*, II, 589.
7 *Journey & Description*, 233-34.
8 Map, Walter, *De Nugis Curialium* [Courtiers' Trifles] ed. and transl. by M.R. James. Rev. by C.N.L. Brooke and R.A.B. Mynors (Oxford, 1983), 183, 197.
9 Llwyd, *Cronica Walliae*, 182.
10 Rowlands, I.W., 'King John and Wales', in Church, S. D. (ed.). *King John: new interpretations* (Woodbridge, 1999), 280.
11 Lloyd, *HW*, II, 590.
12 *BT.Pen.*, 79.
13 *BT.RBH.*, 181.
14 *BT.Pen.*, 80.
15 Quoted in Insley, 'The wilderness years', 168.
16 Lloyd, *HW*, II, 612.
17 *Ibid.*, 614.
18 Rowlands, 'King John and Wales', 278.
19 Insley, 'The wilderness years', 170.
20 *BT.RBH.*, 183.
21 *Journey & Description*, 194.
22 *DWB*, 205.
23 Davies, R.R., *Conquest, Coexistence and Change: Wales 1063-1415* (Oxford, 1987), 294.

IV

Conflict and Co-operation:
Llywelyn and King John, 1201-16

Llywelyn has sworn, and the great men of his land have sworn after him, to observe fealty to King John for ever in respect of his life, limbs and earthly honour.

Llywelyn has received from the justiciar seisin of all the lands of which he was then in possession, to hold until the king's return to England.

After the king's return Llywelyn shall come at his order to do homage to him as his liege lord for the aforesaid lands.[1]

[Terms of the 1201 peace agreement
between John and Llywelyn]

With these words Llywelyn and John sealed their historic agreement. Thus began a fifteen-year relationship between Llywelyn and John that would shift uneasily between friendship and conflict. The period would witness Llywelyn's rise to greatness and John's fall from grace. Although nowhere near as bad as history has portrayed him, John had many failings both as a man and as a king. According to David Carpenter: 'He had betrayed his father and his brother and expected the same conduct from everyone else.'[2] Greed, cruelty, lust and even cowardice have been directed his way both by contemporary chroniclers and modern historians. Nicknames that have attached themselves to John such as 'lackland', 'softsword' and, cruellest of all 'coeur de poupee' (doll's heart), have served to ruin his reputation. (In contrast his brother Richard is remembered as 'coeur de lion' or lionheart). Indeed, Matthew Paris went further than most, declaring that 'Foul as it is, Hell itself is defiled by the foulness of John.'[3] Nevertheless, there are those who see in John the makings of a fine king if not a good man. He is seen as an able military leader, a hard-working administrator, a competent planner and, in spite of his quarrel with the Pope, as conventionally religious. His biographer, the historian Lewis Warren, best sums up the dichotomy that is John inasmuch as he possessed 'the mental abilities of a great king, but the inclinations of a petty tyrant.'[4] This was the man with whom Llywelyn had to do business – a flawed, suspicious but ultimately intelligent and generally able ruler.

THE 1201 PEACE ACCORD

There must have been something in Llywelyn that attracted John, for the king was more willing to court him for a dependant than to crush him out of existence. Less than eighteen months after receiving the king's letters of protection, Llywelyn had become lord of the whole of Gwynedd, including, in the words of J.E. Lloyd, 'Aberffraw, its "principal seat" and its ancient centre, Bangor, the home of its bishop, and Deganwy, the cradle of its ruling house.'[5] This was no longer the quiescent and divided Gwynedd that had first confronted John on his accession; it was a rising power and its ruler was a man who had proved his mettle in war and was about to provide proof of his skill in politics and diplomacy. The first intimation that the English government wished to do business with Llywelyn came in January 1201 when John decided to extend a truce he had concluded with the Welsh prince. Negotiations had gone so well that three months later, in April, Llywelyn was granted a safe conduct to meet John to discuss the terms of a lasting and more formal peace. They did not meet on this occasion because of John's preparations for war and subsequent departure for France in May, but as evidence of the king's desire to secure an agreement with Llywelyn, he did not allow negotiations to lapse and an embassy was dispatched to the frontier. The result was the peace agreement of July 1201.

The principal negotiators, Geoffrey fitzPeter, the king's justiciar, and Hubert Walter, Archbishop of Canterbury, represented, in the words of Ifor Rowlands, 'the sum of Angevin

viceregality during the king's absence in Normandy'.[6] They were
men of wide experience, not least in Welsh affairs, for whom the
king had the highest regard and in whom he had the utmost
confidence. They were men attuned to the demands of running
an 'empire' of which Wales, let alone a northern slice of it, was
but a small, and some might argue, insignificant part. The
Angevin Empire inherited by John covered the greater part of
France and included the overlordship of Wales, Scotland and
Ireland but, arguably, at its heart was England. The inheritance
did not pass to John without a fight for he faced challenges to his
rule from some of his French vassals. Thus, almost from the
beginning of his reign, John was involved in a political and
military struggle to assume mastery of his far-flung dominions.
This explains in part why he hedged his bets in Wales
by appearing to offer, in turn, his protection to Llywelyn,
Gruffudd ap Cynan ab Owain and Gwenwynwyn in 1199. By
1201 the situation in north Wales had become somewhat clearer
with the emergence of Llywelyn and in seeking to establish
relations with this prince, John was pursuing a policy of stability
in one part of his empire while attending to dissident elements in
another.

The 1201 agreement is 'typical of the compacts made with
Gaelic kings, kings of Scots and powerful noblemen of Aquitaine
and elsewhere', but John's appointment of fitzPeter and Walter as
envoys 'who know his mind and are empowered to treat with
Llywelyn', indicates how seriously the king regarded the
enterprise.[7] If this was intended to flatter Llywelyn it may also
have been designed to overawe him. We have no way of
knowing if Llywelyn was overawed; he entered into the
agreement willingly, though he could hardly have failed to be
impressed. According to the terms of the agreement, Llywelyn
swore fealty and became bound into a more formal relationship
with the king whom he acknowledged, via the oath of homage,
to be his overlord and feudal superior. Agreeing to swear oaths of
fealty and homage was entirely conventional and such oaths had
been demanded by English kings of Welsh princes in the past.
However, by agreeing to perform liege homage, the strongest

bond in the feudal world, Llywelyn was entering into a stricter and more binding relationship with the king.

Strictly speaking – and we have no way of knowing how strict an interpretation either party placed on the oath – those from whom kings demanded liege homage were men of status and consequence who invariably held their chief tenements or territories of him, so rendering them his tenants-in-chief. Thus were the nobility, the 'barons', bound to their king to whom they owed allegiance and from whom they received their lands, thus making for a relationship altogether more closely regulated and complex than had characterised that between the Crown and the princes hitherto. This had been demanded of the Welsh only once before, at Oxford in 1177 by John's father, Henry II, of Llywelyn's uncle Dafydd and the Lord Rhys. The difference here is that they were required to swear liege homage in respect of lands held, or claimed, outside their hereditary territories – Gwynedd and Deheubarth respectively – whereas for Llywelyn it apparently included those lands (they are not named in the agreement) that constituted his newly re-assembled principality. Llywelyn had won control of Gwynedd by force and there may have been an element of doubt as to what actually constituted his 'hereditary' lands within it. If this was a concern at the time, the agreement does not show it.

According to Ifor Rowlands, Llywelyn was brought into a 'serviential relationship with the king' as a way of 'normalizing' and formalizing relations between one head of state and another. John largely achieved what his kingly predecessors had sought, namely a clearer and firmer definition of his overlordship, founded on more tangible contracts than were possible with the mere recitation of words which, in spite of the solemnity surrounding their giving, might be conveniently forgotten, deliberately misconstrued or blatantly ignored. If the benefits of the peace are obvious for the hard-pressed John, what did Llywelyn get out of it? At the very least the agreement represented a public acknowledgement by the Crown of Llywelyn's triumph and supremacy over Gwynedd. At most it confirmed and extended the royal protection that Llywelyn had enjoyed since September 1199, thus giving him a valuable breathing space in which to consolidate his power in Gwynedd. In the opinion of Rees Davies, the accord's 'definition of the obligations of dependence has an ominous ring to it' because it required Llywelyn's nobility to swear fealty to the king alongside Llywelyn. In his view the king's overlordship was 'penetrating, as it were, into the political texture of the Welsh principalities.'[8] Winning power was one thing but holding on to it another, and Llywelyn evidently thought the terms of the accord were worth negotiating and ratifying. Whether he intended to follow them to the letter is another matter, nor is it certain that for him, perhaps even for John, the agreement was intended as merely a short-term measure.

Of course to make it binding Llywelyn had to perform in person his liege homage to the king. John did not return to England until December 1203, more than two years after the accord had been agreed. We have no conclusive proof that Llywelyn met the king or that he performed the act of homage but it is widely believed that he did so because in October 1204 John agreed to the betrothal of his illegitimate daughter, Joan, to Llywelyn. The fact that John was at Worcester, a convenient location near the Welsh frontier, a month prior to the betrothal points to a meeting. Indeed, the offer in marriage of his daughter to the Welsh prince suggests that the two rulers were favourably disposed to continuing their cordial relationship for some time to come. So keen was Llywelyn to secure the hand of Joan that he dropped his plans to marry the daughter of Rognvald even though the Pope, after four years of deliberation because she was the widow of Llywelyn's uncle Rhodri, had finally granted permission, in April 1203, for the marriage to go ahead. As A.D. Carr has said, the marriage was 'a dynastic opportunity not to be missed' because 'their children would be part of the European royal and aristocratic network',[9] which is perhaps why Llywelyn so easily put aside his Welsh partner, Tangwystl, the mother of his children Gruffudd and Gwenllian. Llywelyn's marriage with Joan duly took place in the spring of 1205 and it lasted the best part of thirty-two years. Llywelyn's *rapprochement* with John would not last as long, only until 1210, eleven years after they first set out on the road to peace.

THE RIVALRY OF LLYWELYN AND GWENWYNWYN

With John's friendship safely secured and confident of his power-base in Gwynedd, Llywelyn turned to deal with his princely neighbours, the most powerful of whom was Gwenwynwyn ab Owain of southern Powys. The struggle with Gwenwynwyn began in the late summer of 1202 when Llywelyn raised 'a might host' for the conquest of Southern Powys. The reason for this conflict is never made explicit in the chronicles; all the *Brut* says is that 'though he [Gwenwynwyn] was a kinsman to him [Llywelyn] by blood and a near relation, yet he was a man hostile to him in deeds.'[10] What heinous 'deeds' Gwenwynwyn is supposed to have committed is not known, nor can we turn to Gerald of Wales for the answer. All that can be gleaned from Gerald is the apparent suddeness of Llywelyn's attack on Gwenwynwyn 'with whom he had been dwelling in peace.'[11] In fact, Gerald was almost caught up in the conflict for, in travelling to Gwynedd in 1202, he passed through Powys where he found Gwenwynwyn 'on an expedition against Llywelyn'. It is possible that the cause of the quarrel centred on the fate of Maredudd ap Cynan who was expelled from Meirionnydd shortly before Llywelyn's planned attack on Gwenwynwyn. Had the fugitive Maredudd, Llywelyn's enemy, been offered shelter by Gwenwynwyn, an act calculated to anger the prince of Gwynedd? This is a more likely scenario than the one proposed by Humphrey Llwyd in his *Cronica Walliae*, in which he stated that Llywelyn

> callinge to memorye his estate and title, and howe all the princes of Wales, by the ordinnance of Rodrike the Great and after by the lawes of Howell Dha, ought of right to acknowledge the Prince or Kinge of Aberfrawe and Northwales as their liege lorde, and holde their landes of him and non other, and howe of late yeres, by neglygennce of his predecessors they did not use their accustomed duetie . . . therefore called a parliament of

all the lordes of Wales, which for the most part appeared before
him, and swore to bee his liedge men. But Gwenwynwyn
Lorde of Powis wolde not come thither nor take the othe of
alledgyance, which disobedience the Prince declared . . . that
Gwenwynwyn shulde be constrayned, by force, to do his dutie
or els to lose his lande.[12]

Taken literally, this would suggest that Llywelyn was
attempting to impose on the Welsh princes the sort of obligations
that John had demanded of him only the year before. Written
with the benefit of hindsight, Llwyd's chronology is possibly at
fault for it is a scenario more in keeping with what Llywelyn
attempted to do later in his reign than at its beginning.
Nevertheless, there may be some truth in the suggestion that
Llywelyn was beginning to flex his muscles and assert his practical
as well as his theoretical dominance in Wales by emphasizing and
upholding the perceived ancient right and authority of
Aberffraw. As D. Myrddin Lloyd has pointed out, the poet
Llywarch ap Llywelyn 'met the charge of overreaching by
Llywelyn with the assertion that presumption is on the part of
anyone who withstood the claims of Aberffraw's ruler.'[13] The
poet invited the men of Powys to consider who Llywelyn was,
and demanded of them which would be better, having a
'Frenchman' as ruler or a 'generous Welshman'.

Llywelyn's accord with John had enhanced his standing in
Wales to such an extent that he felt confident enough to
summon the lesser princes of north Wales 'to make a solemn pact
to war together against Gwenwynwyn'.[14] The fact that Llywelyn
expected Elise ap Madog, lord of Penllyn, and a member of the
Powysian dynasty, to join him, as his kinsman, suggests the
existence of some form of jurisdictional authority over him. It
also indicates Llywelyn's determination to detach from
Gwenwynwyn any potential allies, especially those who
governed vital border lordships like Penllyn which marked the
frontier between Gwynedd and Powys. In the event the invasion
did not take place partly, it is said, because Elise refused to join
the pact and partly on account of the 'intercession of men of the

Church and laymen arranging peace between Llywelyn and Gwenwynwyn'.[15] Nevertheless, Llywelyn deprived Elise ap Madog of Penllyn though the prince later relented and granted him, 'as charity for his sustenance',[16] the castle of Crogen together with seven townships. This act of mercy was perhaps more apparent than real for it may be seen as a calculated move on Llywelyn's part to demonstrate his power by publicly exercising his lordship by depriving and bestowing lands on those subject to him, by treating Elise, in the words of J.E. Lloyd, 'as a vassal who had fallen short of his obligations to his lord.'[17] What is surprising is that this was done with the apparent approval of Gwenwynwyn, in spite of the fact that a valuable territory had been detached from Powys and added to Gwynedd.

During the next six years, Llywelyn concentrated on strengthening his power in Gwynedd while Gwenwynwyn directed his restless energies to helping Maelgwn ap Rhys reassemble the once mighty Deheubarth which, since the death of the Lord Rhys in 1197, was sadly shorn of its majesty and hoplessly divided between warring brothers and nephews. At the same time, Gwenwynwyn, perhaps unwisely, could not resist making war on his Anglo-Norman neighbours. The Braose family bore the brunt of his attacks and when William (III), the head of the family and, for over twenty years, the leading figure in the Anglo-Norman March, was publicly humiliated and exiled by King John in the spring of 1208, Gwenwynwyn saw this as an opportunity to seize his lordships in mid-Wales, namely, Brecon, Builth, Elfael and Radnor. John took exception to this, especially since these lordships were technically Crown territories on account of their forfeiture, and he summoned the Welshman to a meeting, in October 1208, at Shrewsbury. Gwenwynwyn duly obliged and he, too, was arrested, humiliated and stripped of all his lands. His treatment was what one might expect of a tenant-in-chief being disciplined by his liege lord; this may have been the king's intention, for herein lay the roots of John's policy in Wales to reduce or blur the princes' status by merging them into the feudal background so that they became just some among the mass of his leading noble tenantry.

There was nothing new in this. Welshmen of consequence had long been subject to the processes and pressures of integration, at court, in the church and in other ways such as in marriage, manners and custom, all of which were designed to weave them progressively into the fabric of English politics and society, but John's particular talent was in turning 'process' into 'policy'. For their part the Welsh rulers tended to respond favourably since their increasingly regular and close contact with Marcher lords, the king and his court ensured that much of what they experienced was quickly learnt, imitated and assimilated. Unfortunately for Gwenwynwyn, close contact with the Crown had its downside and, if being humiliated by the king was not bad enough, worse was to follow, for after securing his release by offering oaths of fealty and by handing over twenty hostages, his patrimony was taken from him. Llywelyn took the opportunity to seize southern Powys, in the absence of its lord, effecting an occupation in the space of a few weeks. What Llywelyn had been unable or unwilling to accomplish in 1202 by war, he had achieved in 1208 by politics, speed and not a little help from the Crown.

In not reproving him, John appears to have condoned, if not approved, Llywelyn's annexation of southern Powys. Llywelyn was allowed to keep his considerable prize once he had 'done what he informed the king he would do' in a letter sent to John on 24 December 1208.[18] Unfortunately we do not know what Llywelyn was required to do but he appears to have fulfilled it to the satisfaction of the king who made no mention of his son-in-law's other aggressive act, the defeat and seizure of Maelgwn ap Rhys's lands in Ceredigion. As a close ally of Gwenwynwyn, Llywelyn probably thought it prudent to deal with this scion of the house of Deheubarth before he could react. In a lightning campaign, helped by Maelgwn's retreat and scorched-earth policy, Llywelyn succeeded in prising two-thirds of Ceredigion away from his foe. The cantref of Penweddig he kept for himself but Uwch Aeron he divided between Maelgwn's nephews, Rhys Ieuanc and Owain. As he had done with Elise ap Madog in Powys, deciding the fate of his rulership and territorial power,

Llywelyn was now doing with the princelings of Deheubarth and, thereby, visibly advancing his claims to the overlordship of native Wales.

Why King John should take such an 'indulgent view' of these activities is not easy to explain. Pressures and distractions elsewhere – most notably his quarrel with the Pope over the election of the Archbishop of Canterbury and the continuing machinations of the French king, Philip Augustus – may have led the king to acquiesce in the fait accompli of Llywelyn's territorial aggrandizements.

Indeed, as a mark of the close relations between the two, Llywelyn was invited to join John on his military expedition against the King of Scotland, William 'the Lion', in the summer of 1209. Accompanied by Hywel ap Gruffudd who held Meirionnydd, Gwyn ab Ednywain, his seneschal, and Ystrwyth, his clerk, this was the only occasion on which a ruling prince of Gwynedd joined an English king on a military expedition outside Wales. The conflict was over before it had begun for King William submitted to John without a sword being raised in anger. If the Scottish king had been overawed by the size of John's army, Llywelyn too must have been impressed, for though he was part of it, it may have crossed his mind what might happen if the Angevin military machine were ever turned on him. Ironically, he did not have long to wait for the answer to that question.

LLYWELYN AND JOHN IN CONFLICT

The good relations between Llywelyn and John came to an end in the summer of 1210, when the prince of Gwynedd felt the full weight of his sovereign's displeasure. The breach in their relationship was sudden and not, as far as is known, accompanied by any steady deterioration. That John still regarded Llywelyn with a favourable eye is suggested by his gift of falcons to his daughter and son-in-law in January 1210. Nor, it seems, did Llywelyn show any inclination to test, let alone end, their familial friendship, underlined by his performing homage to John at

Woodstock in October 1209. The reason for the rupture in relations continues to vex historians but the most plausible theories mainly revolve around John's suspicious nature and Llywelyn's lack of judgement.

The fact that John could turn so easily against 'his greatest friend'[19] William III de Braose, may have left a deep impression on Llywelyn. It certainly unsettled and perhaps alienated some of the king's nobility especially if, as David Carpenter has suggested, one of the failings of John's rule was 'the narrowing circle of "ins" and the widening circle of "outs"'.[20] Braose was most definitely out in 1208 for no good reason, according to W.L. Warren, other than John's 'dislike of men simply because they were great and powerful.'[21] John's explanation for his harsh treatment of Braose was the latter's tardiness in paying the Crown the considerable sums it was owed by a well favoured subject. Whatever the reason for the disgrace heaped on the now rebellious Braose – his wife and son were captured and starved to death by John – it is thought that Llywelyn was seduced into supporting the fugitive baron when he, or his adherents, appeared in Wales in the summer of 1210. That some Welsh leaders apparently allied themselves to Braose and his fellow conspirator, his son-in-law Walter de Lacy, is testified by contemporary chroniclers. This does not mean that Llywelyn was among them, nor is it certain the Welsh were fighting in support of Braose who continued the rebellion in Ireland; it may simply have been an excuse for raids of plunder.

Given the king's distrustful nature, Brock Holden may not be far from the truth when he states that 'even if the great Welsh prince himself was not involved, John's suspicion would have been attracted and the king may very well have held Llywelyn responsible for the Welsh attacks of 1210'.[22]

Indeed, unless Llywelyn felt threatened by John's unpredictable behaviour or his so-called 'paranoid nature',[23] to join openly with rebel Anglo-Norman lords would have been a gross error of judgement. Thus, to accuse Llywelyn of showing 'something less than his usual foresight'[24] in making common cause with Braose, may be unfair in the light of the ambiguous

nature of the evidence. On the other hand, it has been suggested
that Llywelyn may have been covertly supporting Braose,
plotting behind the scenes in an attempt to take advantage of the
king's difficulties. It has been suggested that Philip Augustus of
France was stirring up trouble for John by encouraging a wider
rebellion 'by friends and attacks in England, and by friends . . . in
Ireland.'[25] Although Wales is not mentioned Brock Holden
believes that the 'threat of some combination of William de
Braose, the Lacys, and some of the Welsh princes, perhaps
supported by the French, was very real in 1210'.[26] The fact that
Llywelyn concluded a treaty of alliance with the French king in
1212 lends credence to this suggestion. Llywelyn may well have
been tempted to join such a powerful combination especially
since John was distracted by his military campaign to rid Ireland
of the rebels.

The truth is that we simply do not know why John turned
against Llywelyn in the late spring of 1210 but the fact remains
that a large army led by Ranulf III, Earl of Chester, William, Earl
of Salisbury, Geoffrey fitzPeter, the justiciar, and Peter des
Roches, Bishop of Winchester was despatched to north Wales.
The combined status of these individuals indicates the seriousness
of John's intention to deal with Llywelyn. The Crown's forces
penetrated as far as the Conwy where they halted and rebuilt the
castle of Deganwy which, a little time before, Llywelyn 'had
destroyed for fear of the king'.[27] Avoiding direct confontation
with this powerful army, Llywelyn led raids against the enemy
both in the occupied Welsh territories between the Conwy and
the Dee and in the borderland of Chester. Further pressure was
brought to bear on Llywelyn in November 1210 when John,
recently returned from his triumphant summer campaign in
Ireland, restored Gwenwynwyn to southern Powys and
supported Maelgwn ap Rhys's not altogether successful attempt
to recapture those parts of Ceredigion taken from him two years
before. In the spring of 1211, John kept up the momentum of his
attack on Llywelyn by mustering a formidable army of invasion
at Chester. This was to be the first royal campaign undertaken in
Wales for nearly fifty years but John intended that his campaign

should succeed where that of his father, Henry II in 1165, had failed.

Apparently undaunted, Llywelyn, in the words of the *Brut*, 'led frequent attacks against the Saxons, harassing them cruelly'.[28] More seriously for Llywelyn was the king's success in detaching his supporters; leaders such as Madog ap Gruffudd of northern Powys and Hywel ap Gruffudd ap Cynan of Meirionnydd joined Gwenwynwyn of southern Powys, Maredudd ap Rhobert of Cedewain, Rhys Fychan and Maelgwn, sons of the Lord Rhys, to form an impressive native contingent. Only the grandsons of the Lord Rhys, Rhys Ieuanc and Owain, remained loyal to Llywelyn but they were in no position to aid him, being hard pressed themselves in south Wales. In the event, the threatened onslaught did not materialize in large part because the king did not adequately supply his huge army but also on account of Llywelyn's scorched-earth policy. Unable to live off the land or to bring Llywelyn to battle, John's troops began to starve. According to the *Brut*:

> The host suffered lack of food to such an extent that an egg was sold for a penny-halfpenny; and they found the flesh of their horses as good as the best dishes. And because of that the king, having lost many of his men . . . returned in shame to England.[29]

If Llywelyn thought he had weathered the storm, he was wrong. John was more determined than ever to bring his errant son-in-law to heel and less than two months later, at the beginning of July, he was on the border again. This time there was no mistake: the army was larger than before and the supplies were sufficient to meet its needs. The scale of the invasion was such that the oft-used Welsh tactic of withdrawal into the wilderness of Snowdonia simply did not work. John did what no other English king had done before; he crossed the Conwy and, 'destroying all the places he came to',[30] penetrated as far as Bangor. Not even the Bishop of Bangor, Robert of Shrewsbury, was spared the humiliation of being abducted from his cathedral and ransomed for two hundred hawks. The bishop's refusal to meet an excommunicate king was all the excuse John needed to give in to his baser instincts. Llywelyn was in no doubt that unless he submitted without condition, his treatment at the hands of John would be infinitely worse.

The *Brut* makes plain Llywelyn's humiliation, 'being unable to suffer the king's rage' at having to send 'his wife, the king's daughter, to him by the counsel of his leading men to seek to make peace with the king on whatever terms he could.'[31] Granted safe conduct Llywelyn met John not to discuss terms but to listen to them; they were harsh. 'In order to receive the king's grace and good will', the terms of the submission required Llywelyn to cede 'to King John for ever' the Perfeddwlad or Gwynedd Is Conwy, together with the castle of Deganwy; to restore Hywel ap Gruffudd to Meirionnydd; to 'grant the king the allegiance of whichever of his men the king chooses', and to deliver, as a hostage, his son Gruffudd.[32] Llywelyn must have been reeling at this point but John had not yet done, he further demanded tribute; by way of covering his expenses, 10,000 head of cattle, forty war-horses and sixty horses. However, the coup de grâce was surely the king's insistence that if his son-in-law failed to have a male heir by his daughter, Joan, then what remained of the kingdom of Gwynedd would escheat or pass to the Crown on his death. Llywelyn had to be content with his life, liberty, and a realm sufficient in size to enable him to play the part of a prince though with sadly diminished status. Yet even this might be denied him if Ifor Rowlands is correct: 'this clause is novel and suggests that Llywelyn's position in John's eyes approximated to that of a tenant-in-chief in England.'[33]

Having suffered 'the pitiless vengeance of the hardest heart in Christendom', Llywelyn had reached the nadir of his career.[34] For the next ten months Llywelyn duly obliged the king in all his demands, even accepting John's invitation to him and his wife to spend Easter 1212 at the royal court in Cambridge. However, the grandson of the great Owain Gwynedd was made of sterner stuff and, within weeks of celebrating Easter, conflict was resumed. Given the timing of the outbreak of hostilities in June 1212, the planning for war may well have been in hand before the Easter visit. Certainly when war was declared Llywelyn could count among his allies Gwenwynwyn and Maelgwn ap Rhys, men who, a few short months before, had been his implacable enemy. The coalition of native leaders grew as news filtered through of John's cruelty to the Welsh hostages, most notably the sons of Maelgwn, two of whom died after being castrated, and the third, Rhys, was hanged though he was only seven years old. Where John had once craftily balanced one prince against another, he now united them through his cruelty and ambition.

It became clear that John never intended that his Welsh princely allies should replace the prince of Gwynedd, nor did he over-reward them with territory; rather he expected them to accept his overlordship rather than that of Llywelyn. It was, moreover, an overlordship made more rigorous and penetrating by its proximity, for by dint of John's military campaign, occupation of Gwynedd Is Conwy, seizure of the Braose and Lacy lordships and his own landholdings, the Crown's position in Wales was, territorially, larger than it had ever been. To tighten his grip on Wales the king appointed his most trusted servants to positions of power, as in Glamorgan where Falkes de Breaute was made sheriff. As Ifor Rowlands has pointed out, 'this betokened a dangerous and menacing novelty for the Welsh.'[35] The final straw came in the shape of castles, many of which were built at crucial strategic locations, Aberystwyth and Mathrafal among them. In the words of the *Brut*, 'being unable to suffer the injuries which the men from the new castles were inflicting upon' them, the Welsh princes 'rose up against the king'.[36]

Within three months of the outbreak of war, John's castles had either been taken or were closely besieged. This is not to suggest that the Welsh were sweeping all before them; John quickly put an army into the field and succeeded in raising the siege of Mathrafal. Indeed, it soon became clear that John's patience had been tested far enough; this time he intended to encompass the complete destruction of Llywelyn and, arguably, the total conquest of Wales. John assembled a large multi-national force drawn from various parts of his vast continental empire, accompanied by a castle-building contingent of over 8,000 labourers, more than double that recruited by the eventual conqueror of Wales, Edward I. Confident of victory, John assembled his forces at Nottingham and made ready for the expedition. However, the king's confidence was misplaced, for his enemy had been busy negotiating alliances both at home and abroad. The *Brut* makes much of the support offered by the Pope, Innocent III, to Llywelyn and his chief allies in Wales, Gwenwynwyn and Maelgwn ap Rhys, by absolving them from

> the oath and allegiance they owed to the king of England. And he enjoined upon them, for the remission of their sins, to direct friendly endeavour and action against the iniquity of that king.[37]

Emboldened by the papal seal of approval, Llywelyn sought help elsewhere on the continent and found a ready partner in the French king, Philip Augustus. In August 1212 they concluded a treaty of alliance in which they agreed not to make 'truce, peace or even parley with the English.'[38] This was a particular triumph for Llywelyn because the initiative for the alliance may not have come from him but from the French king.

John had clearly miscalculated the scale of the opposition and the extent to which his tyranny had driven some of his own barons to plot against him. In this tense atmosphere of fear and resentment, Llywelyn found a willing cadre of consensual conspirators, men like the exiled bishop of Hereford, Giles de Braose, who may have contributed to the success of the negotiations of the Franco-Welsh treaty. Once acquainted with the news of a baronial conspiracy, John called off the Welsh expedition and prepared to put down the expected insurrections. He succeeded, and for the moment his barons were cowed into submission, but in light of news that Philip's son, Prince Louis of France, was preparing to invade England, John did not revive plans to invade Wales. This gave the Welsh the vital breathing space they needed and during 1213 they scored significant successes by capturing the castles of Deganwy and Rhuddlan along with the four *cantrefi* of Gwynedd Is Conwy. The best the

Crown could muster was a token gesture in the shape of an English fleet ordered to sail around the north Welsh coast and, where possible, land raiding parties to inflict as much damage as possible. Bereft of ideas on how to contain the Welsh, John resolved to revive an old expedient by seeking out rivals of Llywelyn and encouraging them to challenge for the rulership of Gwynedd. The two hapless nominees were Llywelyn's cousins, Owain ap Dafydd and Gruffudd ap Rhodri, sons of his late uncles. Neither was given any practical or material support to aid their cause, which was lost before it had begun.

Pressed on all sides, John decided, in May 1213, to make peace with the Pope, do the penance demanded of him and accede to the appointment of Stephen Langton as Archbishop of Canterbury. In becoming a papal vassal, and making England a papal fief, John sundered the alliance between Llywelyn and Innocent III but not before the latter negotiated, via his papal legate Pandulf, a truce between them. In agreeing to the truce, Llywelyn was guilty of breaking the terms of his alliance with Philip of France who alone was left to face the full fury of the English king. However, John's French campaign of 1214 to recover Normandy did not go as planned and his defeat at the battle of Bouvines in July gave fresh impetus to baronial conspiracies in England. The crisis facing John was such that he abandoned his earlier attempts to divide the Welsh by seeking instead to win them over to his cause. Hostages were released, demands for the return of the castles and territories taken by the Welsh were dropped and overtures in the form of peace proposals were offered via William, the Bishop of Lichfield, who came in person to the border to meet Llywelyn and his princely allies. John's promises fell on deaf ears; Llywelyn was in no mood to compromise with a king he simply did not trust. Aware of the possible advantages for Wales should a baronial faction force the king into making concessions, Llywelyn promptly sided with John's enemies. Thus did the native chroniclers report the events dominating the first half of 1215:

> And that strife spread so much that all the leading men of
> England and the princes of Wales made a pact together against

the king that no one of them, without the consent of all the
others, would make peace or agreement or truce with the king
until . . . there should be restored to each one of them their
laws and their power and their castles, which he had taken
from them without law or truth or justice.[39]

It is possible that Llywelyn had already been courted by
Archbishop Langton, who was responsible for extending the
papal truce, and by Bishop Giles de Braose, whose brother
Reginald was sent to Wales with instructions to aid the Welsh in
their attempt to recover control of the Braose lordships of
Brecon, Radnor, Builth, and Blaen Llyfni. In a further move to
cement the alliance between Llywelyn and the Braose family,
Reginald agreed to marry the prince's daughter, Gwladus.

As the resistance of the barons grew stronger, John became
more stubborn and desperate; civil war was inevitable. In May
1215 the dissident barons, led by the earls of Essex, Hereford and
Norfolk, seized London. John and his baronial supporters, the
earls of Chester, Derby, Salisbury and Pembroke had been
outmanoeuvred. As London fell to the rebels, Llywelyn marched
on Shrewsbury (prompting some historians to suggest a co-
ordinated military campaign) taking both the castle and the town
without a fight. The taking of Shrewsbury was a significant act
on the part of a Welsh prince and must not be underestimated,
for Shrewsbury, along with Chester and Hereford, symbolized
English power on the border. The duration of the town's
occupation is not recorded but it is likely that once hostilities had
ceased and peace established, it would have been returned to the
Crown. Of course, one cannot rule out the possibility that
Llywelyn intended that the town should be used to bargain with
the king. Within weeks, John had been forced to the negotiating
table at which time the barons invited Llywelyn to join them and
benefit from the concessions they intended to wrest from a
reluctant king. This is not to suggest that the dissident barons and
their princely allies were working in effective combination; there
might still have been an element of distrust between them.

LLYWELYN AND MAGNA CARTA

Magna Carta is probably the best-known document in the English language. Yet apart from the odd grandiloquent phrase and clause the so-called 'Charter of Liberties' is, in essence, a functional, even mundane, treaty intended to establish peace between the king and his subjects. In negotiating the terms of the Charter, Llywelyn managed to secure concessions embodied in three 'Welsh' clauses, namely, the return of lands or liberties of which he and his fellow Welsh princes had been unjustly deprived; the freeing of all hostages, including Llywelyn's son, Gruffudd, with immediate effect; and the cancellation of all charters unfairly extorted from the Welsh princes particularly that which Llywelyn was forced to agree to in the bleak summer of 1211. In cases of dispute, it was agreed that there should be trial according to English, Welsh, or marcher law, depending on the status and location of the lands or liberties claimed. These demands, set alongside the fifty-eight other clauses drawn up by the barons, were submitted to John on 15 June and were reluctantly accepted by him.

Llywelyn was not present at Runnymeade so it became necessary for him and his princely colleagues to meet John if the terms of the Charter were to be made binding. At the end of July a council meeting was arranged at Oxford whereby John could meet his barons and ratify the terms of the Charter. The Archbishop of Canterbury, Stephen Langton, appears to have been entrusted with the task of overseeing Welsh affairs. He arranged a safe-conduct and escorted Llywelyn and his allies to the council to meet the king. Langton's mediation may have been instrumental in gaining further concessions from the king, for in addition to the terms agreed in the Charter, and as if to emphasize Llywelyn's status and standing in Wales, John made a grant to his son-in-law of the manors of Bidford in Warwickshire and Suckley in Worcestershire. This was a beneficient act on John's part that perhaps signalled a more penitent approach to dealing with the prince of Gwynedd. We do not know how long Llywelyn remained at Oxford but it is likely that once negotiations had been concluded he returned to Wales.

It is possible that Llywelyn, with Langton's active co-operation, took the opportunity to discuss wider issues beyond those agreed in Magna Carta. The appointment of two Welshmen to the vacant bishoprics of Bangor and St David's during the Runnymeade conference is certainly worthy of note and may be more than mere coincidence. The see of St David's had been vacant for some time due, in part, to John's insistence that his nominee, Hugh Foliot, be elected its bishop and, partly, as a result of the resistance offered by the cathedral canons. They wished to elect Iorwerth, abbot of Talley, a 'man of worthy character and a pure Welshman by birth.'[40] According to T. Jones Pierce, Iorwerth's election was a 'triumph of policy for Llywelyn', and while we might agree with this conclusion it does not take into account the possible influence of the most powerful landowner in the diocese, William Marshal, earl of Pembroke.[41] A supporter of John during the recent civil war, Marshal was a pragmatist who may have persuaded the king to concede Iorwerth's election knowing that, as the Crown-appointed keeper of the temporalities in south-west Wales, he would be in a better position than Llywelyn to influence, if not control, the new bishop. Of greater importance to Llywelyn was the election of the Bishop of Bangor, a diocese that lay almost entirely within his orbit of power. The election of Cadwgan, Abbot of Whitland, almost three years after the death of the last bishop was a victory that may be attributed directly to Llywelyn's influence.

CONFLICT RENEWED

The spirit of reconciliation engendered by the sealing of the Charter did not outlast the summer. There were some among the barons who believed the king had not been humbled sufficiently and they were reluctant to give up their gains. Even as they gathered at Oxford suspicion began to grow on both sides and it became clear that the peace between the king and his barons would not long survive. The intervention of the Pope proved pivotal when he denounced the Charter as 'shameful and base but also illegal and unjust'.[42] Innocent's denunciation served to cripple the power of the church, and especially Langton, to act as mediator. By September 1215, war had broken out and the more truculent barons took the decisive step of inviting Prince Louis of France to be their king in the hope that he would bring a French army to their aid. There is no evidence to suggest that Llywelyn was party to, let alone knew of the barons' intention to war with John. Nor had the Welsh prince been in contact with his erstwhile ally, the French king. This war, it seems, was entirely a civil one and took no account of the views or opinions of the Welsh. One result of the king's difficulties was to give fresh vigour to Llywelyn who aimed to take advantage of the chaos in England to further his cause in Wales.

It was not until three months after hostilities in England had been renewed that Llywelyn opened his campaign. In a rare move he opted to conduct his military operations outside the usual campaigning season, that is spring and summer, and appeared at the head of an army making for south Wales in early December 1215. This had the advantage of surprising the castle garrisons which probably did not expect to be attacked during the winter months. Fortunately for Llywelyn, 'so great was the mildness of the air and the fine weather that a winter as mild as it was never seen nor heard of before that'.[43] It was not only the weather that impressed itself on the native chronicler; the overwhelming success of the campaign was clearly a cause for celebration, 'and all the princes, happily jubilant, returned victorious to their own lands.'[44] The castles captured by Llywelyn and his allies read like a travelogue; they included Cydweli, Llanstephan, St Clears, Laugharne, Narberth, Newport, Cardigan and Cilgerran. However, the prize was Carmarthen, for nearly a century the centre of royal power in south-west Wales which was surrendered to Llywelyn after a five-day siege. If the English chronicler Roger of Wendover can be relied on, it seems Llywelyn was employing terror tactics to aid his military campaign. According to Wendover, the Welsh prince 'beheaded all the people he found'[45] in those castles which resisted him, most notably Carmarthen.

In an impressive show of unity, Llywelyn was joined by his cousins Hywel ap Gruffudd ap Cynan and Llywelyn ap

Maredudd ap Cynan, Gwenwynwyn of southern Powys, Maredudd ap Rhobert of Cedewain, Rhys Gryg, Maelgwn ap Rhys and the sons of Gruffudd ap Rhys from Deheubarth, and the household troops or *teulu* of Madog ap Gruffudd of northern Powys. The sheer scale of the Welsh military machine deployed to support Llywelyn, 'the most powerful force in Wales'[46] according to Sean Davies, may well have convinced some garrison commanders to submit and retire with their lives if not their goods. This campaign was a landmark event in Llywelyn's career since it was the first occasion on which he had led the majority of his fellow Welsh princes in battle and it was his first appearance as a war-leader in south Wales. It has been suggested, with good reason, that between 1215 and 1217 the Prince of Gwynedd wielded so much military power that 'no Marcher army dared to face Llywelyn ap Iorwerth in the field.'[47] In fact some of those same Marcher leaders were either related or allied to Llywelyn: the Braose lordships in mid-Wales were in the possession of Reginald, Llywelyn's son-in-law, while the earldom of Glamorgan was ruled by the dissident Earl of Essex, in right of his wife Isabella. The anglicized heartland of southern Pembrokeshire alone held out for the king and English power under the leadership of the redoubtable William Marshal. Yet even Marshal, according to his biographer David Crouch, 'could do little more than sit tight and try to hold what he could.'[48] In fact, Marshal was hard pressed elsewhere in south Wales particularly in Gwent where 'his lands had been much battered by the Welsh prince Morgan ap Hywel', Lord of Caerleon, who had 'gravitated into the political orbit of Llywelyn ap Iorwerth'.[49] Clearly, no part of Wales was immune to Llywelyn's influence.

THE COUNCIL OF PRINCES AT ABERDYFI, 1216

In 1216 Llywelyn resolved to demonstrate and exercise his power over the other Welsh princes when he summoned them to a council at Aberdyfi. The focus of the meeting was very firmly directed towards ending the squabbling of the princes of Deheubarth. For nearly twenty years, since the death of the Lord

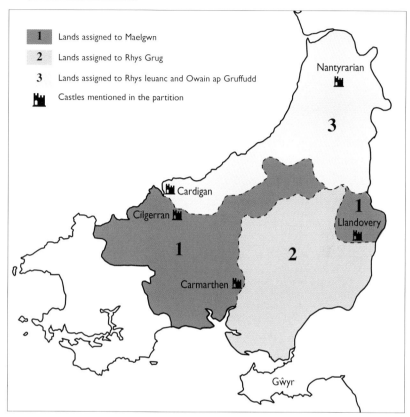

1 — Lands assigned to Maelgwn

2 — Lands assigned to Rhys Grug

3 — Lands assigned to Rhys Ieuanc and Owain ap Gruffudd

Castles mentioned in the partition

Nantyrarian

3

Cardigan

Cilgerran

1

Llandovery

1

2

Carmarthen

Gŵyr

The partition of Deheubarth as agreed at the assembly of princes at Aberdyfi in 1216.

Rhys in 1197, Deheubarth had been racked by civil war so Llywelyn took it upon himself, with the consent of 'the leading men of Wales . . . and all the learned men of Gwynedd',[50] to resolve the conflict by partition. Each of the sons and grandsons of the Lord Rhys was apportioned a share of the kingdom. This ensured that Deheubarth would remain divided and under the control of Llywelyn who made his intention to police the arrangement crystal clear. The success of his arrangement may be measured by the fact that it remained in force and unchallenged for the rest of his reign.

Acting in the role of statesman, Llywelyn wisely refrained from claiming a share of the partitioned Deheubarth for himself.

Nevertheless, it is probable that he exacted some kind of oath of allegiance, perhaps even an oath of homage, from his fellow princes who now became subject to him. This might explain why Gwenwynwyn, in the words of the *Brut*,

> renounced and scorned the oaths and pledges and charters which he had given to Llywelyn ap Iorwerth and to the princes and the leading men of Wales and England, and he renounced the homage he had done to Llywelyn and the hostages whom he had given to him.[51]

Vexed and angry, Llywelyn tried a conciliatory approach by sending

> bishops and abbots and other men of great authority to him, and with them the tenor of the cyrographs and the charters and the pact and the homage which he had done to him, to beseech him to return.[52]

Gwenwynwyn remained unmoved and counted on the support of the man who had persuaded him to defect, namely, King John. As part of his stratagem to entice Gwenwynwyn away from Llywelyn's allegiance, the king restored to Gwenwynwyn the manor of Ashford in Derbyshire (granted to him in 1200), and added the important manor of Montgomery. Hard pressed by his enemies in England, John did nothing to help Gwenwynwyn except encourage his flight to the safe custody of the Earl of Chester. If John thought Gwenwynwyn could somehow challenge Llywelyn in Wales or stir up dissension among the Welsh leadership he was dangerously out of touch. Gwenwynwyn was a spent force and, unable to 'reconcile himself to the defeat of all his ambitions',[53] he died in exile later that same year. Llywelyn moved to occupy southern Powys, which he intended to hold for longer than he did the last time he annexed the kingdom.

The assembly of magnates that met at Aberdyfi is important because it was the first of its kind but whether we can credit it as 'virtually a Welsh parliament',[54] as J.E. Lloyd does, is debatable. It certainly marked Llywelyn's emergence as a prince of native Wales in all but name. In the opinion of J.Beverley Smith, the Aberdyfi meeting was significant because the Welsh leaders who participated, especially those of the partitioned Deheubarth, 'were accommodating themselves in a new political association.'[55] A new political structure was created in which the supremacy of Gwynedd was acknowledged and the relationship between the princes was changed from that of allies of Llywelyn to being his vassals. Indeed, by the summer of 1216, Llywelyn controlled more of Wales than any Welsh ruler had done since the time of Gruffudd ap Llywelyn in the mid-eleventh century. Despite his gains, Llywelyn was by no means safe from the unwelcome attention of a desperate King John who appeared on the Welsh border, in July 1216, seeking allies to aid him in his war against the army of Prince Louis of France, which had landed in England some six weeks before. The king sought to woo both Llywelyn and Reginald de Braose but, as the *Brut* gleefully put it, though the king 'begged of them to be reconciled to him in every way . . . they would not have it'.[56] As the civil war raged in England, Llywelyn concentrated on consolidating his power in Wales.

Events took a sinister turn in October 1216 when John fell ill and suddenly died leaving a nine-year-old child, his son Henry, as his heir. Should Prince Louis triumph, Llywelyn would be faced with the prospect of peace but with the uncertainty of having to deal with a new, and potentially more powerful, adversary. On the other hand, if the barons loyal to John's son, Henry, succeeded in restoring the power of the Crown, that power might, for many years, be weaker and not as menacing as it had been during the previous reign. Llywelyn did not intervene but awaited the result of the war with a detachment that belied the significance of the final result. He spurned an invitation to take part in the election of the new king and did not attend the coronation of Henry III at Gloucester. This suggests that he did not wish to be drawn too deeply into the vortex of English political power. As a seasoned political operator, Llywelyn may have reasoned that to accept the invitation might be interpreted by some as a sign of his acceptance of the Crown's desire to reduce the ruler of Gwynedd to the approximate status of an English baronial tenant-in-chief. Llywelyn was determined to secure peace from a position of strength with whichever side won the civil war.

Notes

1 Pryce, Huw (ed.). *The Acts of Welsh Rulers, 1120-1283* (Cardiff, 2005), 371-2.
2 Carpenter, D.A., *The Struggle for Mastery : Britain 1066-1284* (London, 2003), 266.
3 Giles, J. A. (transcr.), *Matthew Paris' English History (with a continuation) from 1235 to 1273* (3 vols., London, 1852-4), II, 669.
4 Warren, W.L., *King John* (2nd. Edn., London, 1978), 258-9.
5 Lloyd, *HW*, II, 613.
6 Rowlands, I. W., 'The 1201 peace between King John and Llywelyn ap Iorwerth'. *Studia Celtica*, 34 (2000), 150.
7 *Ibid.*, 154.
8 Davies, *Wales 1063-1415*, 294.
9 Carr, *NewDNB*, online edn.
10 *BT.Pen.*, 83.
11 *The Autobiography of Giraldus Cambrensis*, ed. H.E. Butler (Rev. edn., Woodbridge, 2005), 249-50.
12 Llwyd, *Cronica Walliae*, 186-7.
13 *Guide to Welsh Literature*, 179.
14 *BT.RBH.*, 185.
15 *BT.Pen.*, 82.
16 *BT.RBH.*, 185.
17 Lloyd, *HW*, II, 614.
18 *AWR.*, 377-8.
19 Holden, Brock W., 'King John, the Braoses, and the Celtic fringe, 1207-1216', *Albion*, 33:1 (2001), 5.
20 Carpenter, *Britain 1066-1284*, 274.
21 Warren, *King John*, 184.
22 Holden, 'King John, the Braoses', *Albion*, 33:1 (2001), 19.
23 Warren, *King John,* 249.
24 Lloyd, *HW*, II, 632.
25 Holden, 'King John, the Braoses', *Albion*, 33:1 (2001), 18.
26 *Ibid.*, 18.
27 *BT.Pen.*, 84.
28 *Ibid.*, 85.
29 *Ibid.*, 85.
30 Giles, J. A. (transl.). *Roger of Wendover's Flowers of History, A.D. 447-1235* (2 vols., London, 1849), II, 58.
31 *BT.Pen.*, 85.
32 *AWR.*, 386-7.

33 Rowlands, 'King John and Wales', 282.
34 Norgate, Kate, *John Lackland* (London, 1902), 286.
35 Rowlands, 'King John and Wales', 284.
36 *BT.Pen.*, 87.
37 *Ibid.*, 87.
38 *AWR.*, 392.
39 *BT.Pen.*, 89.
40 *DWB.*, 416.
41 *Ibid.*, 416.
42 Warren, *King John,* 245.
43 *BT.Pen.*, 92.
44 *B.Saes.*, 213.
45 Davies, Sean. *Welsh Military Institutions, 633-1283* (Cardiff, 2004), 245.
46 *Ibid.*, 217.
47 *Ibid.*, 126.
48 Crouch, David B., *William Marshal : court, career and chivalry in the Angevin Empire, 1147-1219* (London, 1990), 114.
49 *Ibid.*, 127.
50 *BT.Pen.*, 92.
51 *Ibid.*,
52 *Ibid.*,
53 Lloyd, *HW*, II, 649.
54 *Ibid.*
55 Smith, *Llywelyn ap Gruffudd*, 18.
56 *BT.Pen.*, 93.

V

Belligerence and Bargaining:
Llywelyn and King Henry III, 1216–34

King Henry III. From his tomb effigy in Westminster Abbey.
(Dean and Chapter of Westminster Abbey)

> Llywelyn has sworn on relics at Worcester before the
> legate Guala and King Henry . . . to strive to ensure that
> all the magnates of all Wales will come on a fixed day
> and at a fixed time to do homage and fealty to the king
> as their liege lord, just as they or their predecessors did
> to the father of the king and his predecessors.[1]
>
> [Terms of the 1218 peace agreement between
> Henry III and Llywelyn]

The sealing of this agreement was, arguably, more important for Llywelyn than that sealed seventeen years earlier with King John. Llywelyn was older, wiser and in a far stronger position than he had ever been. The fact that the Crown expected Llywelyn to mediate between it and the other Welsh princes points to a tacit acknowledgement of his supremacy in native affairs. On the other hand, the Crown was subject to a minority, divided by civil war and weaker than it had been for some time. Indeed, Roger of Wendover thought the reign of the boy-king, Henry III, was doomed since the French 'were confident that they had the kingdom of England in their power'.[2] The recovery and eventual victory of the Crown by 1217 owed much to the leadership of two men: the regent, William Marshal, and the justiciar, Hubert de Burgh. The aged Marshal had long been an adversary of Llywelyn but de Burgh had yet to lock horns with the wily Welsh prince.

De Burgh's first appearance in Wales can be reliably dated to 1201 when King John invested him with the custody of the Three Castles of Gwent and the power to safeguard the southern Welsh border. Replaced in 1205 by William de Braose, de Burgh was employed on other more significant missions for a king who came to value his services. In 1215 John appointed him justiciar, a post he continued to hold after the king's death and during the crucial first sixteen years of Henry III's reign. So powerful did he become that the scribe of the Waverley Abbey annals stated that 'He lacked nothing of royal power save the dignity of a royal diadem.'[3] Therefore, although he was not present, it is likely that de Burgh was chief among those in the young king's government – including Guala the papal legate, and William Marshal – who were the inspiration behind the terms of the 1218 peace negotiated with Llywelyn.

A 'tough and ruthless graduate of the school of King John',[4] de Burgh was thrusting, ambitious and, like the late king, the victim of character assassination. He has been accused of having a 'darker side', which made possible his poisoning of William Marshal the younger, his betrayal of the young William de Braose, and his self-aggrandizement. It has been claimed that he aimed to establish a 'principality' in south and mid Wales to rival that of Llywelyn in the north, but if that was his intention it made little impression on the native chroniclers who seemed oblivious to his presence. The jury is still out on de Burgh but one thing is certain, he proved to be a most formidable adversary for Llywelyn.

THE TREATY OF LAMBETH, 1217

In September 1217 the civil war was concluded in favour of John's son Henry III. The French under Prince Louis had been vanquished, the dissident barons brought to heel and the Welsh made an offer of peace. The result was the treaty of Lambeth, a peace that satisfied the majority of the participants but not the Welsh, who would have been required to surrender all their territorial gains. Clearly, this was unacceptable and Llywelyn did not respond to these overtures of peace but continued his destructive military campaign that had begun three months earlier in June. The cause of this renewal of hostilities was Reginald de Braose's repudiation of his alliance with Llywelyn and his reconciliation with the Crown in the Treaty of Kingston. Angered by what he considered to be his son-in-law's betrayal and worried by the defection of other former Marcher allies – Peter fitzHerbert, Thomas Corbet of Caus, John Fitzalan and Fulk fitzWarin – Llywelyn moved quickly to secure the Braose lordships in south-east Wales. Llywelyn's army overran the lordship of Brecon, captured the town and then made for Gower. The campaign was so swift and effective that Braose 'came, and six knights along with him, and surrendered to Llywelyn'.[5] Llywelyn entrusted the captured Braose castle at Swansea to the care of his ally, Rhys Gryg of Deheubarth. After a few days' rest, a combined army of northern and southern Welsh swept west and lay siege to the town and castle of Haverfordwest. Unable to obtain the support of their lord, William Marshal, the men of Pembrokeshire sued for peace and, with the aid of Iorwerth, bishop of St David's, came to terms with Llywelyn. According to the *Brut*, they should give twenty picked hostages from Rhos and Pembroke, against their giving him by the feast of Michael [29 September] a thousand marks of silver, or else that they should surrender themselves to him to hold their land and territory under him.[6]

It is perhaps significant that terms of a financial nature were looming large in Llywelyn's negotiations – a hundred marks in silver had been demanded weeks earlier from the townsfolk of Brecon – which may indicate a need to fund state-building activities such as castle construction.

Satisfied with his gains, Llywelyn returned 'joyfully' to Gwynedd. William Marshal was anything but joyful and in a determined attempt to oust the Welsh from Caerleon in Gwent he laid siege to the castle. He succeeded. Meanwhile, in the south-west, Rhys Gryg completed the conquest of the lordship of Gower and in so doing

> drove all the English away from that land and took from them of their chattels as much as he pleased; and he drove with them their wives and children without a hope of their ever returning. And he divided their lands for Welshmen to occupy.[7]

It is hard to imagine Rhys Gryg undertaking a campaign in Gower without either the knowledge or consent of Llywelyn. The fact that Rhys was allowed to maintain his grip on this critically important lordship for over two years suggests that Llywelyn was quite prepared to allow his allies some freedom of action. On the other hand, the attack on Gower may have been a calculated response to Marshal's siege and capture of Caerleon castle, held until then by Llywelyn's Welsh allies in Gwent. These events, coupled with the bold and independent action taken by Llywelyn, caused some concern at the king's court, where it was decided that some form of accommodation must be reached with the Welsh.

THE PEACE OF WORCESTER, 1218

In March 1218, Llywelyn was persuaded to meet the king's representatives at Worcester to discuss peace terms. Under a safe conduct he did so and, in a series of agreements, concluded the terms of what became known as the Treaty of Worcester. In the opinion of A.D. Carr, 'The peace of Worcester was a cessation of hostilities rather than a treaty, but it underlined Llywelyn's supremacy.'[8] Mediated with the help of the papal legate, Guala, some, though not all, of Llywelyn's territorial conquests since 1212 were confirmed, as was, crucially, his custody, during the king's minority, of the strategically important royal castles of Cardigan and Carmarthen. His custody of southern Powys (along with the royal castle of Montgomery) was likewise confirmed though he was drawn, somewhat reluctantly, to accept that its possession would be reconsidered when Gwenwynwyn's heir, Gruffudd, came of age. Equally uncongenial was the pledge that Llywelyn was required to give in respect of restoring some of the conquered Marcher lands to their former lords. The Marcher families of Braose, Mortimer and Marshal were among the worst affected by the dispossessions, which caused them to be particularly aggressive in their determination to recover their lost territories. More importantly, perhaps, is the fact that the Crown did not undo (nor did it confirm) the territorial arrangements Llywelyn had made at Aderdyfi in respect of the dynasty of Deheubarth. In return, Llywelyn agreed to accept the overlordship of the Crown, pay homage to the king and, significantly, promise to persuade the other Welsh princes to do likewise.

The terms of the peace were, generally speaking, favourable to Llywelyn but fell far short of his ultimate ambition. Llywelyn's aim was to turn a military alliance of Welsh princes, of which he was head, into a permanent political arrangement. This required him to persuade the Crown to relinquish its direct relationship with the Welsh princes in favour of one in which he, Llywelyn, would act as an intermediary between the two sides. In short, Llywelyn wanted the Welsh princes to do homage to him and he alone to do homage to the king of England. Initially it looked as if Llywelyn might be granted his wish, for he alone of the princes of Wales was invited to negotiate with the Crown's representatives in Worcester. However, as J. Beverley Smith pointed out, the Crown was prepared to acknowledge Llywelyn's leadership and the influence which he exercised upon the princes, but they were 'his allies rather than his tenants; he was their leader, not their lord.'[9] Llywelyn was made an agent of the Crown and entrusted with the responsibility of bringing 'the princes back into their old allegiance' in which each of them was required to do homage and fealty to the king as before.[10] This proved easier to command than to accomplish; as the *Brut* explains, 'Rhys ap Gruffudd alone of all the men of the South, by counsel of the Lord Llywelyn, made for the king's court and did him homage.'[11] Neither Rhys Gryg nor Maelgwn ap Rhys showed the slightest inclination to fulfil the terms of the treaty agreed by their overlord Llywelyn. The Crown's reaction was to tread softly and not stir up trouble, preferring instead to rely on the cooperation and goodwill of Llywelyn or, as J.E. Lloyd put it, he was 'to be humoured and pacified rather than coerced.'[12]

MAINTAINING THE PEACE

Maintaining the peace proved difficult and it soon became clear that trouble could not be avoided. In August 1220, barely two years after the Worcester peace negotiations, Llywelyn felt compelled to punish Rhys Gryg for refusing to do homage to Henry III and for not surrendering the Marcher lordships of Carnwyllion, Gwidigada, Cydweli and Gower when commanded to do so. Why Rhys, alone of Llywelyn's allies, should be forced to concede Marcher territory is not easy to determine. Clearly, Llywelyn had to appear to be complying with the least digestible terms of the Worcester peace agreement and in targeting Rhys Gryg, he may have found a way in which to satisfy the one whilst disciplining the other. It is possible that Rhys may have begun to entertain notions of grandeur that were beyond his ability to fulfil. Llywelyn's telling reference to the vanished glories of Dinefwr – 'once famous and now in ruins, to which the privileges of all South Wales once belonged'[13] – may indicate an intention on the part of Rhys to restore the greatness that was once Deheubarth. It is noteworthy that some months earlier, in 1219, Rhys had taken to wife the daughter of Gilbert de Clare, earl of Gloucester, one of the three most powerful Marcher lords in Wales. As Lord of Glamorgan, Clare's territory bordered that of Gower the newly acquired lordship of his son-in-law. Llywelyn may have feared a deliberate attempt on the part of Rhys to form an alliance with the Clare family that might serve to bolster the latter's claim to Gower and other territories in south-west Wales.

Rhys Gryg's marriage, and possible alliance, had implications for Llywelyn who had given his daughter, Margaret, in marriage to John de Braose. A nephew of Reginald de Braose, John, who had only recently been released from a long captivity, laid claim to the Braose estates in Wales, a move that had excited Llywelyn who saw the possibility of involving himself in the dispute. Partly to avenge himself on Reginald and partly to gain another Marcher ally, Llywelyn supported John de Braose's claim and granted him the former Braose lordship of Gower. The Crown was certainly unimpressed since it had decided in favour of Reginald de Braose and expected Llywelyn to hand Gower to him. Llywelyn, however, did as he pleased and not what the Royal Council wished. Rhys Gryg's reluctance to give up Gower and the other lordships brought Llywelyn south with an army to compel him to comply. As Llywelyn intended, Gower was given to John de Braose, but in an effort to pacify Rhys and maintain the support of his southern Welsh allies, the lordships of Cydweli and Carnwyllion were restored to the prince of Dinefwr.

Having brought Rhys Gryg into line, Llywelyn now turned west to Pembrokeshire to deal with William Marshal the younger who had succeeded his father on the latter's death in 1219. Where the elder Marshal had shown restraint in dealing with Llywelyn, his son did not. The younger Marshal was determined to recover lands lost to the Welsh and would not wait for

Llywelyn to comply with the terms of the peace of Worcester. Twice Llywelyn met representatives of the Crown at Shrewsbury, in July 1219 and May 1220, to discuss the vexed issue of returning Marcher territory, but little had been achieved. In the second of those meetings, Llywelyn had come to an agreement with Marshal whereby a truce was concluded and another meeting was set for August to hammer out terms. However, Llywelyn did not appear and, as the chroniclers report, Marshal, or his men, responded 'by making frequent attacks upon the Welsh and harassing them'.[14] In a week-long campaign Llywelyn succeeded in capturing the castles of Narberth and Wiston, and burning the town of Haverfordwest up 'to the gates of the castle.'[15] Marshal's men were cowed into submission and forced to agree to a humiliating truce. An indignant Marshal demanded action and, belatedly, in October, the Crown responded by rebuking Llywelyn and summoning him to appear at Worcester. Llywelyn did not appear and the Crown did not punish him.

Marshal's frustration with Llywelyn's intransigence and the Crown's apparent impotence was shared by a fellow Marcher Lord, Hugh Mortimer. Under the terms of the Peace of Worcester, Mortimer fully expected Llywelyn to hand back the lordship of Maelienydd but after some prevarication, Llywelyn eventually rejected his claim. Llywelyn instead declared his support for the ruling dynasty, his allies, the sons of Maelgwn ap Cadwallon, namely, Cadwallon and Maredudd, because they were simply recovering territory taken from them by the Mortimers. Mortimer's appeal to the Crown evidently fell on deaf ears since the lordship remained in Welsh hands until Llywelyn's death. On a happier note for Llywelyn, his meeting in Chester, in August 1220, with his former adversary, Earl Ranulf, went well and the two came to a mutual understanding. They agreed to resolve the dispute over the custody of Mold castle and to arrange a marriage alliance between the two families. Thus, Llywelyn's occupation of the border fortress was confirmed and, in 1222, the prince's daughter, Helen, was married to Ranulf's nephew and heir, John the Scot.

Hardly had Llywelyn resolved these problems, partly by force and partly by negotiation, than he was inundated with news of intrigue. According to the *Brut*, 'strife arose' between Llywelyn and his eldest but illegitimate son, Gruffudd, over the latter's seizure of the cantref of Meirionnydd. The seriousness of the conflict between father and son is related in vivid detail by the native chroniclers:

> Llywelyn took that subjugation angrily; and he gathered a host and went against Gruffudd and threatened to avenge that attack heavily upon him and upon his men. And Gruffudd, having arrayed his troops ready to fight, boldly awaited the coming of his father.[16]

The prospect of civil war horrified the Welsh nobility and, the 'wise men on either side' promptly intervened to stop the conflict escalating out of control. Gruffudd was urged 'to surrender himself and all his possessions to his father's will' whilst Llywelyn was advised to receive his errant son 'peacefully and mercifully, and to remit to him all his anger from a good heart'.[17] War was averted and, having dispossesed his son of Meirionnydd, Llywelyn built the castle of Y Bere to safeguard his power in the lordship. A possible cause of Gruffudd's bitter conflict with his father may have been due to Llywelyn's success in having his younger legitimate son, Dafydd, acknowledged as his heir by the Crown at the Shrewsbury meeting in May 1220. Peace between father and son reigned once more but it left a bitter taste in the mouth and the strength of the familial relationship would be tested again.

With Gruffudd pacified, Llywelyn faced trouble again from the princelings of Deheubarth, this time in the person of Rhys Ieuanc, nephew of Rhys Gryg. According to the native chroniclers, Rhys

> quitted the fellowship of the Lord Llywelyn, for he was angered because Llywelyn had given the castle of Carmarthen to Maelgwn ap Rhys and had not given to himself the castle of Cardigan, which had before that come to him from the apportioning of the lands of Deheubarth.[18]

Having witnessed his uncle's discomfiture at Llywelyn's hands a year earlier, Rhys Ieuanc determined to seek powerful allies and in William Marshal of Pembroke he found one. Alarmed at the prospect of a hostile Anglo-Welsh alliance in south-west Wales, Llywelyn moved swiftly to dispossess Rhys of his lands and capture the castle of Aberystwyth. Rhys repaired to the king's court to seek redress of his grievances and a meeting was called at Shrewsbury to which Llywelyn was summoned to appear. At the beginning of July 1221, Llywelyn answered the summons and came in person to settle his dispute with Rhys Ieuanc. It is likely that Llywelyn realised his error in not dealing fairly with Rhys and conceded the issue at Shrewsbury; both Cardigan and Aberystwyth castles were either bestowed on, or restored to, Rhys. Rhys Ieuanc died in the August of the following year at which point Llywelyn, acting ostensibly in the guise of the king's agent, took control of the deceased's lands, and, in default of a direct heir, divided them between Owain ap Gruffudd, Rhys's brother, and Maelgwn ap Rhys, his uncle.

WAR WITH MARSHAL AND DE BURGH

Llywelyn's volte-face at Shrewsbury did not harm his prestige within Wales or his standing outside the country. Rather it was a triumph of common sense over pride and stubbornness, for Llywelyn was well aware that his best interests lay in avoiding a serious breach with the Crown. Although brinkmanship was a ploy used regularly by Llywelyn he seemed to know instinctively when to draw back from the edge. However, early in 1223 Llywelyn acted contrary to his usual caution when he crossed the Shropshire border and took the castles of Kinnerley and Whittington. The reason why Llywelyn launched this cross-border attack is never made clear, but it may have had something to do with the Crown's granting permission, in June 1221, for the fortification of at least one, if not both, castles. The fact that Whittington was the property of Fulk fitzWarin, a former ally who had betrayed Llywelyn by defecting to the Crown after the death of King John, may be significant. Indeed, the timing of the attack may have been deliberate and designed to seize the castles as their refurbishment, over a period of eighteen months, neared completion.

The Crown reacted with alarm and a force under the justiciar, Hubert de Burgh, made haste for Shrewsbury. Conciliation rather than retribution was the preferred policy of de Burgh and attempts by Ranulf, Earl of Chester, to mediate in the dispute were welcomed on both sides. However, before a settlement could be agreed, events elsewhere took a sinister turn when, according to the *Brut*, 'William Marshal brought a large fleet and a multitude of knights and foot-soldiers from Ireland to Deheubarth'.[19] Within a fortnight of his landing, in April 1223, Marshal had taken the castles of Cardigan and Carmarthen. He also regained the lordship of Emlyn and its castle of Cilgerran. Llywelyn's son, Gruffudd, was sent south with an army to do battle with Marshal who duly obliged. After a hard but, in the opinion of the native chroniclers, inconclusive battle fought at the bridge over the Tywi just below Carmarthen castle, Gruffudd was forced to withdraw north for lack of supplies. Interestingly, the English chronicler, Roger of Wendover, contradicts his Welsh counterparts by declaring the battle a victory for Marshal. With pardonable exaggeration Wendover claimed that the Welsh were put to flight, hotly pursued and near 9,000 of them slain without mercy.

According to the native chroniclers, Llywelyn met Marshal, the king, his justiciar and the Archbishop of Canterbury at Ludlow to discuss terms but no such meeting is otherwise recorded. Successive attempts were made to secure a meeting but Llywelyn remained defiant and he may have begun to suspect that Marshal and de Burgh were secretly collaborating. Certainly, de Burgh did nothing to censure Marshal for his attack on the Welsh, nor did he condemn the seizure of the fortresses of Cardigan and Carmarthen. In fact, R.F. Walker believes that there is sufficient evidence to suggest that de Burgh came to the Welsh border 'already prepared for war'.[20] In what was clearly a well-planned operation, Marshal inflicted a severe reverse on Llywelyn whose authority in south-west Wales ebbed away.

Local Welsh rulers began to defect and throw in their lot with Marshal, among them the grandsons of the Lord Rhys, namely, Cynan ap Hywel Sais and Rhys Mechyll ap Rhys Gryg.

In July 1223, de Burgh gave up any pretence to impartiality and, judging Marshal's campaign to be in the royal interest, openly sided with the Earl of Pembroke. The Earl of Salisbury was appointed by de Burgh to command a troop of cavalry intended to support Marshal in military operations in south Wales. Llywelyn's response was two-fold; to send his son Gruffudd south to deal with Marshal and Salisbury, while he undertook the siege of Reginald de Braose's castle of Builth. Supported by Rhys Gryg, whose son had joined the enemy, Gruffudd and a 'mighty host'[21] could do little to stop Marshal taking the castle and lordship of Cydweli and a large swathe of southern Ceredigion. Gower too was threatened and John de Braose was faced with the unpalatable prospect of having to choose between the English Crown and his father-in-law, Llywelyn. Meanwhile de Burgh struck in mid-Wales, firstly to raise the Welsh siege of Builth and, secondly, to secure Montgomery, build a new castle there and wrest control of southern Powys away from Llywelyn. To aid him in his enterprise, de Burgh released Owain and Gruffudd, the sons of Gwenwynwyn, from their detention in Bridgnorth Castle. They were entrusted with the task of taking the allegiance of the men of Powys away from Llywelyn for which their reward would, doubtless, have been a half-share each of their late father's kingdom.

Llywelyn soon came to the conclusion that the forces arrayed against him were too formidable to engage, and although his position in north Wales was not yet in danger, he realised that unless he sought terms, his allies in the south – Rhys Gryg, Owain ap Gruffudd, and Maelgwn ap Rhys – ran the real risk of losing everything in his cause. A truce was agreed and at Montgomery, in October 1223, Llywelyn and his principal allies met de Burgh and the Royal Council. The terms were harsh but not overly so, nor were they unexpected given the scale of Llywelyn's defeat. It was demanded of Llywelyn that he should restore his Shropshire conquests, Kinnerley and Whittington, to their righful owners, give up all claims to the castles of Cardigan and Carmarthen, surrender Cilgerran to Marshal and return Montgomery to the Crown. For its part, the Crown agreed to restore the lands taken from Llywelyn's southern allies provided they could substantiate their claim in law. To facilitate this a joint Anglo-Welsh commission was proposed whereby all claims and counter-claims could be debated. As a result, between 1223 and 1225, Marshal returned southern Ceredigion to Maelgwn ap Rhys but Llywelyn's other allies in Deheubarth were forced to cede control of the lordships of Cydweli (to de Londres), Cemais (to FitzMartin), St Clears, Llansteffan and Laugharne. The winner by far in this redistribution of power in south Wales was William Marshal whom the king appointed to be his royal bailiff of Cardigan and Carmarthen. In addition, Marshal's custody of the lordship of Emlyn with its castle of Cilgerran was confirmed and his marriage with Eleanor, the king's sister, was quickly approved and arranged.

For ten years after 1212, Llywelyn had hardly set a foot wrong but 1223 proved to be a turning point inasmuch as the Welsh prince acquired two implacable foes in William Marshal the younger and Hubert de Burgh – 'the one having an unsatisfied grievance against the prince, the other having observed at first hand the ineffectiveness of English diplomacy.'[22] The loss of Cardigan and Carmarthen dented Llywelyn's ambitions in the south and damaged his credibility among the princelings of Deheubarth. A swift but careful recovery was essential and when, in 1224, opportunities presented themselves in the shape of the Lacy rebellion in Ireland, which Marshal was sent to crush, and the flight to Wales of the rebel Falkes de Breaute, Llywelyn refrained from involvement. This is not to suggest that Llywelyn was cowed and subdued, far from it, as his written communications with the king demonstrate, but he likely thought it prudent to risk nothing by further acts of aggression. When the Crown demanded that Llywelyn give up Falkes de Breaute, the prince declined to comply insisting, in a letter to the king of July 1224, that he had 'as much liberty as the king of Scotland, who receives outlaws from England with impunity.'[23] According to Huw Pryce this was 'a significant indication of the prince's political aspirations, and reflects his readiness to use written communications with the crown as a means of talking up his status.'[24] Unable to contemplate a conventional war with weapons, Llywelyn entered into a war of words. Becoming ever more statesmanlike in his dealings with foreign as well as domestic authorities, Llywelyn realised that the written word could be as effective a tool as the sword, as his treaty with the French king, Phillip Augustus, and letters to Popes Innocent III and Honorious III, ably demonstrated.

Although Llywelyn's action in receiving Falkes de Breaute was contrary to the terms of the Peace of Worcester – he had explicitly promised not to receive the Crown's enemies – his reply was dignified if disingenuous:

> The king should not feel angry that Falkes went to Llywelyn. Llywelyn would make greater efforts towards ensuring a reconciliation between Falkes and the king if the king's council allowed justice to be done to Falkes. Indeed, Llywelyn has more to complain of in this regard than Falkes. Not only are Llywelyn's rights not given him, but great losses are dishonourably inflicted on him. Though he does not impute anything to the king himself, Llywelyn has no hope that the king's council wishes to make satisfaction to him. Llywelyn has complained so often that he is ashamed to recall his grievances, since he has had no satisfaction for them.[25]

It is clear that Llywelyn's target was Hubert de Burgh and not his brother-in-law, the young Henry III, whom he was careful not to blame for his grievances. Given the problems confronting the Crown at this point – the renewal of civil war seemed inevitable – de Burgh did not react to Llywelyn's accusations nor did he seek to punish the prince for breaking the terms of the peace. De Burgh appeared content to see the prince powerful, as long as his power led to no disturbance in either Wales or the March. For his part Llywelyn exercised his authority cautiously but wisely making plain his intention to protect his Welsh princely allies in the south. This he did without recourse to conflict when, early in 1225, he sent envoys to London to plead the case of Maelgwn ap Rhys, whose lands in southern Ceredigion were being subjected to the unwarranted, and aggressive, attention of William Marshal's officers. His success may be judged by the fact that a commission was convened not only to investigate the dispute but to make inquiry and begin the process of partitioning the lands between Maelgwn and his nephews, Cynan ap Hywel and Owain ap Grufudd, both of whom had been allied to Marshal and in opposition to Llywelyn in the war of 1223.

Seeing that he could not persuade either Llywelyn or Ranulf, Earl of Chester, to support his rebellion, de Breaute did not remain long in Wales. In fact, by 1225 his rebellion was over and he was forced to quit the kingdom, while that of his confederate in Ireland, Hugh de Lacy, had been crushed by Marshal. More gratifying for Llywelyn was news of the deaths of two enemies of old, Hugh Mortimer in 1227 and Reginald de Braose in 1228, and, more especially, the decline in the fortunes of his arch-enemy William Marshal who fell out with the king's justiciar, de Burgh. His success in Ireland notwithstanding, in 1226 Marshal was stripped of some of his authority in Wales most notably his custody of Cardigan and Carmarthen. However, as Marshal's influence in Wales declined, that of de Burgh increased but not so that Llywelyn felt threatened. In fact, the three years between 1224 and 1227 were a period of comparative quiet, during which conflict was avoided both by Llywelyn and the Crown. As if to emphasise their cordial relations, no fewer than four meetings were held between Llywelyn or his representatives and the representatives of the Crown, in Worcester and Shrewsbury between September 1224 and August 1226. Official pleasantries and gifts of land and birds of prey were exchanged, but as far as Llywelyn was concerned the most significant results of those meetings were the papal legitimization of his wife, Joan, and the king's consent to the Welsh princes taking an oath of fealty to his son, Dafydd.

MONTGOMERY AND THE CERI CAMPAIGN

The good relations between Llywelyn and the Crown were shattered in September 1228 when war was resumed. The cause of hostilities is not clear but it may have had something to do with the king's generous grant of the strategically significant castle and lordship of Montgomery to Hubert de Burgh in April 1228. This investment in the power and prestige of the king's justiciar in the March was a challenge that Llywelyn could simply not ignore. It had become clear to the prince that the end of his brother-in-law's minority (Henry III declared himself of age in January 1227) had enhanced rather than diminished de Burgh's authority, who, by dint of the king's trust and confidence, became, in the words of J.E. Lloyd, 'the real governor of the realm'. In fact, Lloyd was confident that the conflict 'was not provoked by any aggression on the part of the Welsh leader', but was almost entirely due to de Burgh's overweening ambition.[26] R.F. Walker has disputed this version of events, stating that to blame the outbreak of war on de Burgh's 'alleged ambition to gain "a vast marcher lordship" in Wales', is unfair. He is equally dismissive of A.H. Williams's assertion that in clearing the woodland south of the castle of Montgomery, de Burgh was intentionally encroaching on the neighbouring lordship of Ceri, which was to be used as 'a stepping-stone to further acquisitions'.[27]

If anything, the outbreak of war was due to a combination of factors, of little significance in themselves, but when added together, formed a formidable raft of reasons for conflict. For example, the reduction of the forest boundary between Montgomery and Ceri, the only natural defence the latter possessed, and the trespass by de Burgh's men in Ceri caused friction, as did the apparently unprovoked attack by local Welshmen on English merchants in royal service. In a less heated atmosphere, each could be explained away and the problems resolved. Given the difficult nature of the terrain, the clearing of woodland to facilitate the construction of a roadway seems entirely logical as does the trespass by the justiciar's men, which was as likely accidental as intentional. The fact that Llywelyn sent a letter of apology to King Henry III in connection with the assault on the merchants suggests that the prince had no hand in that affair. Nevertheless, petty local quarrels in the March had a habit of drawing great men into their orbit and, given the Crown's increasing frustration with Llywelyn, whom it accused of political prevarication and diplomatic infidelity, war between the king and the prince on a grand scale seemed inevitable.

Indeed, signs of strain in the relationship between Crown and prince were evident months before the outbreak of war. In March 1228, a month before the grant of Montgomery to de Burgh, the king had confiscated the two English manors – Rothley and Condover – which it had granted to Llywelyn's wife Joan only a year or two before. Llywelyn certainly seemed reluctant to meet the king and his justiciar and by the summer of 1228 he had not done so for two years. When a conference was arranged in Hereford for August, Llywelyn sent his wife to negotiate an extension of the truce that had kept the peace for over three years. Ironically, when Llywelyn did eventually agree to meet the king, at Shrewsbury on 10 September, the anticipated conference was scuppered by the outbreak of hostilities a week before. In what R.F. Walker describes as 'a reproachful and coldly hostile letter',[28] Henry III made plain his anger with Llywelyn whom he blamed for breaking the peace. If the English chronicler, Roger of Wendover, is to be believed, hostilities opened with a Welsh attack on Montgomery castle. This would certainly explain why the king and de Burgh hastened to the area to relieve a besieged fortress. If Llywelyn had planned this attack then he would indeed have been guilty of breaking the peace, but it is just as likely that local Welsh leaders acted on their own initiative. When war began, Llywelyn was not in the vicinity, nor did he arrive with his forces until days later.

When it came, war was neither on a grand scale nor was it decisive. The king and de Burgh seemed content to move no further into Wales than the border lordship of Ceri, which they occupied and set about defending by building a castle. The conflict devolved into a series of skirmishes rather than the set-piece battle favoured by the English and in one of these 'fierce attacks' which 'caused great confusion',[29] William, the son of Reginald de Braose, was wounded and captured by the Welsh. Within three weeks the 'war' was over, diplomatic relations were resumed and peace terms were negotiated. It was agreed that Ceri should be restored to its Welsh ruler on payment of a relief, and that Llywelyn should pay a sum of £2,000 in reparations. For his part, Henry III undertook to respect the boundary between Montgomery and Ceri, once a commission appointed to the task had properly defined it, and to destroy the half-built castle of his justiciar, which became known as Hubert's Folly. The king confirmed de Burgh's custody of Montgomery castle and assisted his justiciar in meeting the costs of its refurbishment.

As royal expeditions go, this was a complete fiasco; at great cost to the Crown in terms of organisation, time and finance, little had been accomplished. The king and de Burgh seemed content to conduct a static campaign of occupation and construction. This made them prey to Welsh raids and skirmishes, a tactic used to devastating effect by Llywelyn. Exactly what the king and de Burgh intended to achieve, beyond flexing their collective muscle, is a matter for debate. Certainly, contemporary chroniclers were at a loss to excuse the expedition's failure. Roger of Wendover suggested that a serious lack of food supplies was the primary cause of failure but this is not borne out by the evidence gleaned from royal Chancery records, which reveal an army that was well fed, watered and munitioned. One native chronicler was in no doubt that the 'vast host of the might of England' had been assembled for one purpose only, namely, 'to subdue the Lord Llywelyn and all the Welsh.'[30]

However, the conquest of Wales was probably not on the royal agenda, but if the king and de Burgh had expected to overawe Llywelyn with a demonstration of the power of the English military machine, a task undertaken with considerably more skill and gusto by King John in 1211–12, they had seriously underestimated their foe. It was as if the king and de Burgh lost interest once Llywelyn made plain his intention to resist the

Crown's forces. Perhaps they had expected more from their Welsh allies, the dispossessed sons of Gruffudd ap Gwenwynwyn, who, the scribe responsible for compiling the near-contemporary *Cronica de Wallia* states, had been encouraged by the Crown with promises of restoration to their late father's kingdom, in order to foment rebellion against Llywelyn in neighbouring Powys. Arguably, the most telling evidence is that furnished by Matthew Paris, who put the expedition's failure down to dissension within the royal ranks caused, in the main, by jealousy of, and hatred for, de Burgh.

The failure of the Ceri campaign was a serious blow to the reputation and authority of de Burgh but he remained a force to be reckoned with. Llywelyn, on the other hand, came out of the affair with his reputation intact and, if Matthew Paris is to be believed, he had cause to be a little less fearful of the justiciar thereafter. Nevertheless, de Burgh's power in Wales was enhanced rather than diminished when the king, who continued to trust and favour his justiciar, granted him the royal lordships and castles of Cardigan and Carmarthen, and entrusted him with the homage and service of Llywelyn's son-in-law, John de Braose, for the lordship of Gower. Eighteen months later, in November 1230, on the death of Gilbert de Clare, de Burgh was granted custody of his heir, Richard, and the Clare lordships of Glamorgan and Gwynllwg. Thus, de Burgh had become the most powerful Marcher lord in Wales at a time when he continued to dominate the government of Henry III under whose guidance, according to one English chronicler, 'the royal will waxed hot and fervent.'[31]

Llywelyn was not unmindful of the justiciar's continuing presence in both Wales and the English government but he was certainly not overawed. Indeed, the fact that he was confident enough to adopt a more forceful and authoritative title when, in May 1230, he began to style himself 'Prince of Aberffraw and Lord of Snowdon' bespeaks a consciousness of power that extended far beyond the borders of his native Gwynedd. He was no longer simply prince of north Wales but, as the new style suggested, was now de facto prince of native Wales. He stopped short of adopting the title Prince of Wales because he wished to secure the acknowledgement and ratification of the Crown, which, at this juncture, was unlikely to be forthcoming. Nevertheless, the Crown was anxious to maintain cordial relations with Llywelyn, which may explain why, in October 1229, Henry III met Dafydd at Westminster and received his homage. Significantly, the terms by which Dafydd rendered his homage made plain the Crown's recognition of him as Llywelyn's lawful successor. Not only that: the king also granted his nephew an annuity of £40 with the promise of further grants of land. The future looked bright but dark clouds were soon to come into view that had the potential to destroy his achievements.

BETRAYAL AND EXECUTION:
  JOAN AND WILLIAM DE BRAOSE

If, as J.E. Lloyd believes, 'Llywelyn had come through the troubles of 1228 with flying colours',[32] he was soon brought low by the revelation that his wife of twenty-five years had been unfaithful. As one might expect, details of this clandestine affair are sparse but the incident was thought to be of sufficent merit to be noted by the native chroniclers, one of whom stated that Braose 'had been caught in Llywelyn's chamber with the king of England's daughter, Llywelyn's wife.'[33] The seeds of betrayal were probably sown in the autumn of 1228 when William de Braose, Llywelyn's prisoner, was first brought to the court of the Welsh prince and there met Joan. His war wounds may have required a special care that could more fittingly be provided by Llywelyn's wife and her female attendants. As the young nobleman was brought back to health, Llywelyn negotiated his ransom with the Crown and a sum of £2,000 was agreed. It is perhaps no coincidence that the sum corresponded precisely to that which Llywelyn had agreed to pay to the king in reparations following the end of the ill-fated Ceri campaign.

In the spring of 1229, after a captivity lasting some six months, Braose was released but not before Llywelyn had obtained from him binding promises that he would never again bear arms against the prince, and, more significantly, that he would give his daughter, Isabella, in marriage to Dafydd. This marital arrangement would be of vital importance for the future of Gwynedd for it would not only bind Llywelyn's designated heir in blood to one of the most powerful Marcher families in Wales, the third such marriage to be negotiated; but it would also bring with it, as Isabella's dowry, the strategically significant lordship of Builth. Indeed, as matters stood (and unless William had a son) the Braose patrimony faced the very real prospect of being divided upon his death among his four daughters. If the marriage went ahead Dafydd could, therefore, expect to share in the property apportioned to his wife as one of the four co-heiresses. Of all the things that could go wrong and stand in the way of fulfilling this carefully thought-out scheme, 'a cruel domestic crisis' was perhaps the least expected.

The storm broke at Easter 1230 when Braose paid a visit to Llywelyn's court, presumably to finalise the details of the marriage alliance and, perhaps, to negotiate the release of the companions and servants who had been captured alongside him in Ceri in the autumn campaign of 1228. How long Braose had been at court before he and Joan were discovered in compromising circumstances is not known, but immediately upon their detection they were separated and imprisoned. Within a month of his detention William was tried before a council of Llywelyn's magnates, found guilty and sentenced to death. According to Nicholas, Abbot of Vaudey, William de Braose was

> hanged from a tree in a certain manor called Crokein [Crogen near Bala] on the morrow of the feast of Philip and James [2 May 1230], in the presence of more than eight hundred persons, called together for the lamentable spectacle, especially those who were enemies of William de Braose senior and his sons.[34]

How or why the prince's suspicions were aroused is not made clear but to accuse Hubert de Burgh, as Roger of Wendover does, of deliberately supplying the information on which Llywelyn was forced to act is probably unfair and owes more to the chronicler's vindictive imagination than to truth. Indeed, J.E. Lloyd was of the certain opinion that 'it was the outraged husband, not the astute politician, who hanged William de Braose.'[35] This is a sentiment shared, more recently, by Kari Maund who stated that 'this was not the action of a diplomat' but of a man acting 'without thought, in anger and distress.'[36] In short, this was a simple tale of marital infidelity rather than of political intrigue.

Nevertheless, there is an air of conspiracy about the affair that can not easily be dismissed. Certainly, some contemporary annalists thought the whole incident a ploy conjured up by Llywelyn to falsely accuse Braose and justify his murder. More recently, Huw Pryce has expressed the possibility that Llywelyn may well have 'welcomed the prospect of the fragmentation of a great Marcher lordship among William's heiresses, one of whom was engaged to marry his son and designated successor, Dafydd.'[37] If this was so then Llywelyn was playing for high stakes and ran the very real risk of jeopardizing the whole arrangement. His letters to Eva de Braose, William's widow, and her brother, William Marshal, Earl of Pembroke, reveal a prince eager to ensure the continuation of the marital arrangements. To Eva, Llywelyn wrote the following:

> To inform him whether she wishes the alliance between his son Dafydd and her daughter Isabel to stand, for it will never rest with Llywelyn that it should not stand. If she does not wish this, she will wish to inform him of her will regarding the alliance and the right of her daughter so that nothing worse can result from the misfortune.[38]

To Marshal, Llywelyn wrote asking

> The earl to inform him whether he wishes the friendship between the earl's niece and Llywelyn's son Dafydd to stand; . . . and assures him that he does not wish their friendship ever to be broken because of this or of anything else in the world.[39]

To both, Llywelyn expressed his regret that he 'could not have prevented the magnates of his land from making the judgement they made, knowing the punishment for the dishonour and insult to him.'[40] In fact, his magnates simply 'would not bear not having passed the sentence on William' because he had 'plotted to deceive [him] bringing him dishonour beyond measure by deceitfully entering his chamber.'[41] Clearly, Llywelyn was at pains to treat the matter as one affecting William only, a view that was evidently shared not just by the executed's widow and brother-in-law, but also by the Crown. The marriage went ahead and the Crown's only response to Braose's execution came in a letter to Llywelyn three months later, in August 1230: it referred to the 'mischance which befell him.'[42] This does not indicate a lack of interest on the part of the Crown but is probably a reflection of its current difficulties in France. The king had begun a major continental campaign to regain his lost French dominions, which explains why Henry was distracted and needed to maintain peace in Wales. Perhaps the most interesting feature of the affair is the way in which Llywelyn and his nobility confidently assumed that they had the right to try, judge and execute a man who was a subject of the English Crown. The Crown apparently did not challenge Llywelyn's jurisdiction in the matter though how this was expressed in legal terms – by means of Welsh, English or Marcher law – is not known.

WAR AND THE FALL OF HUBERT DE BURGH

Llywelyn's execution of William de Braose was passed over in virtual silence in England and did not contribute to the outbreak of hostilities in 1231. The cause of that conflict has been hotly debated but, as yet, no satisfactory answer has been forthcoming. J.E. Lloyd had no doubt that the 'renewal of strife' was due 'to the ill-will with which Llywelyn saw the justiciar attempt to build up for himself a mighty power in South Wales.'[43] He was referring to the fact that during 1231 the king entrusted the custody of the Braose lands to de Burgh, thus augmenting his already extensive land holdings in Wales. However, R.F. Walker disagrees, stating that Llywelyn opened hostilities before de Burgh was given responsibility of administering the Braose patrimony. If anything, the timing of Llywelyn's initial attack in the neighbourhood of Radnor followed hard on the heels of the news of the death, in April 1231, of William Marshal, Earl of Pembroke. In spite of Llywelyn's protestations of friendship in his letters to the earl, Marshal had remained a dangerous foe. The fact that custody of the Braose lordships had first been granted to Marshal, within weeks of their lord's execution, may well have alarmed Llywelyn. This may explain why the prince moved quickly to take control of the lordship of Builth before his son's marriage had taken place (Builth had been promised to Dafydd in fulfilment of his bride's dowry). Since Marshal was on campaign with the king in France he could do nothing until his return; in his absence, the administration of the extensive Braose territories was entrusted to his seneschal, William fitzAdam.

The maintenance of peace between Llywelyn and William Marshal was made more difficult and precarious by the inevitable feuds that grew up between their respective local officials. There were unsettled questions that demanded resolution, not the least of which was the legality of Llywelyn's occupation of Builth. Although this issue was apparently resolved at a meeting held at Shrewsbury, in June 1230, between Llywelyn and the king's regents, the chancellor, Ralph Neville, bishop of Chichester, and Stephen Segrave, this agreement did little to lessen the friction that had developed between the rival seneschals of Brecon and Builth, William fitzAdam and Gwyn ap Goronwy respectively. Gwyn ap Goronwy was certainly vigorous and aggressive in defence of Llywelyn's rights and it was, in part, his provocative conduct that led to conflict between the men of both lordships. In a letter of September 1230 to the king's regent, Ralph Neville, fitzAdam complained that although

> he has kept all the men of Brecon so quiet that none of them
> crossed the border of Builth to do evil there, Llywelyn's men
> have once, twice and thrice entered the land of Brecon, and
> have taken away by force plunder from the men of that land.[44]

Gwyn ap Goronwy was apparently keen to secure the freedom from custody of Madog Fychan, the son of Einion

Fychan, one of Llywelyn's principal officials, but fitzAdam was unwilling to agree. The seneschal of Builth was adamant that unless Madog was freed then 'he [fitzAdam] will be choosing war and will certainly have war.'[45] The appointment of an arbitration commission in the autumn notwithstanding, war came six months later, in April 1231, when, according to Roger of Wendover, Llywelyn attacked Radnor. This attack may have been in response to the king's order that Radnor, along with a host of other border fortresses, be garrisoned immediately and that merchants refrain from trading with the Welsh of the region, especially in weapons and food. The force of Llywelyn's attack was blunted somewhat when in May the king came to the border to negotiate a truce. Safe conducts were issued to encourage Llywelyn to send envoys to Worcester to discuss peace terms but none came. After a month of posturing, during which the Welsh ceased their attacks on frontier fortresses, Henry III left the border and headed for London.

Almost as soon as the king departed, sometime early in June, Llywelyn struck, first at Montgomery where he destroyed the town but failed to take the castle, and then at Radnor and Hay-on-Wye, where he destroyed the castles and towns. By the end of June, the Welsh campaign had stepped up a gear and Llywelyn's forces were ranging far and wide, assaulting Brecon, besieging Caerleon and threatening Newport. Soon they turned westward, taking Neath and Cydweli, destroying their castles and towns, and laying siege to Cardigan. According to the *Brut*, Llywelyn and his southern allies, the princelings of Deheubarth, took Cardigan after only a brief siege lasting days during which 'they breached it with catapults, till the garrison was forced to surrender the castle and to leave it.'[46] According to Roger of Wendover, Llywelyn's campaign was mobile and highly successful but the Welsh did suffer some reverses most notably at Montgomery where a raiding party was cut to pieces and the captured beheaded.

The Crown responded to the Welsh insurgency by excommunicating Llywelyn and by preparing a large military expedition. By the beginning of August, the royal forces were on the border but it soon became evident that the strategy to be adopted was that followed three years earlier in Ceri. The king's great campaign against the Welsh did not lead to much fighting or to much marching. The army moved cautiously into Wales, covering some twenty miles, before it stopped at Painscastle in the lordship of Elfael. Here it settled down and set about the task of re-building in stone an existing earth and timber fortress intended to forestall any future Welsh aggression in this region. It has been suggested that the choice of Painscastle was made because of its 'nearness to Llywelyn's recent acquisition of Builth' but it may also have been intended to secure the lordship of Elfael, part of which had been occupied by the prince some months earlier. The English army encamped around the fortress for some two months, venturing only occasionally into neighbouring lordships to harass the Welsh. Detachments were sent to support and re-supply castle garrisons in the region but there were no large-scale engagements. Politically and militarily there was stalemate, a fact that did not impress some English chroniclers, such as the scribe from Dunstable priory who wrote, with pardonable exaggeration, 'while the king rebuilt Painscastle, Llywelyn destroyed ten castles on the marches of Wales'.[47]

The king and his commander-in-chief, Hubert de Burgh, failed to draw Llywelyn into a decisive battle; nor did they succeed, either through bribe or treachery, in detaching his allies from the prince. In fact, it is difficult to see what de Burgh had intended to achieve with this expedition for no sooner had the royal forces left Wales than Llywelyn raided those areas recently occupied by the Crown. If de Burgh had hoped to pressure Llywelyn into negotiaitng a peace similar to that achieved at Worcester, he was to be disappointed. Llywelyn showed not the slightest inclination to come to the negotiating table in the weeks following the abortive royal expedition. In fact, he had probably achieved his objective inasmuch as he needed to flex his muscles from time to time to remind his allies and clients that he was still a force to be reckoned with. The fact that the majority of the Welsh princes joined him in the campaign shows how vigilantly he exercised his authority. In the south east, Llywelyn was supported by the native rulers of Morgannwg, Hywel ap Maredudd and Morgan Gam, and the Lord of Senghenydd, Rhys ap Gruffudd. In the south west, the young Maelgwn Fychan joined with his uncle, Rhys Gryg, and cousin, Owain ap Gruffudd, to assist Llywelyn in the siege of Cardigan.

Neither Henry III nor de Burgh could dislodge the prince from his comfortable position as the arbiter of domestic and dynastic politics in native Wales. A plan to mount a new expedition in the spring of 1232, supported by naval attack on Anglesey with forces recruited in Ireland, came to nothing. Consequently, at the end of November, a year's truce was concluded in which it was agreed that a more permanent peace be negotiated the following year. Negotiations were resumed in the spring but no lasting peace was forthcoming. The scene was set for the fall of Hubert de Burgh. He had built a reputation as a soldier so his military failure in Wales in 1231, coupled with that of 1228, had seriously damaged his standing at court. Worse still was his failure to organise properly the king's military expedition to France, which contributed to its failure. De Burgh's enemies sensed their prey weakening and once the king's trust had been broken they moved in for the kill. His wealth, royal favour and autocratic manner made enemies of powerful men, principal among them Peter des Roches, Bishop of Winchester, his nephew (or son), Peter de Rivallis and Stephen Segrave. During 1232 a power struggle ensued in which de Burgh was ousted from office and replaced by Segrave while Bishop Peter became the king's chief adviser.

Although Llywelyn played no part in de Burgh's downfall, he must have rejoiced at the disgrace of his old adversary. Of more immediate concern was the question of who would succeed de Burgh in Wales. The answer was not long in coming when Peter de Rivallis was granted the former justiciar's possessions. Llywelyn had little time to bask in the glow of de Burgh's disgrace for news reached him of the death of his chief ally, Earl Ranulf of Chester. For some years Llywelyn had been secure in the knowledge that this great border earldom posed no threat to his eastern frontier. It was fortunate therefore that Ranulf's successor, John the Scot, was Llywelyn's son-in-law, a nobleman who proved to be as friendly to Gwynedd as had been his predecessor. Hardly had Llywelyn come to terms with the demise of Earl Ranulf when he was informed of the accidental death of his other son-in-law, John de Braose. Since John's son and heir, William, was a minor, his lordship of Gower, together with its principal castle at Swansea, passed to the Crown until he came of age. The king's decision to grant custody of Gower to Rivallis must have concerned Llywelyn inasmuch as he had yet to measure the resolve of his new adversary. However, as events were to show, Llywelyn need not have worried for Rivallis was soon removed from power and his Welsh territories were confiscated.

REBEL ALLIANCE: LLYWELYN AND RICHARD MARSHAL, EARL OF PEMBROKE

The fall of de Burgh and the rise of Bishop Peter did not lead to the cessation of rivalries in the English court. Riven by noble faction and paralysed by political friction, the king's government was challenged by Richard Marshal, Earl of Pembroke. According to Roger of Wendover, Marshal 'fought for the cause of justice, and the laws of the English race against the oppression of the Poitevins', the king's foreign favourites.[48] Marshal's rebellion was a godsend for Llywelyn who took advantage of the unrest in England to stamp his authority on the March. Early in 1233 he responded to the rebuilding of Radnor castle by the king's brother, Richard, Earl of Cornwall, by launching an attack on the neighbouring lordship of Brecon. Here Llywelyn 'manfully laid siege to the castle of Brecon every day for a whole month with catapults, and he threw the walls to the ground.'[49] After destroying the towns of Clun and Oswestry, Llywelyn returned to his own lands, carrying 'many spoils away with him',[50] and satisfied that he had demonstrated to the Crown the perils of fortifying castles on his borders.

A few short months later the king marched into Wales at the head of a large army, not to punish Llywelyn but to pursue

Marshal. The king laid siege to Usk castle, held by Marshal's ally, Walter de Clifford, but failed to take it. This failure convinced the king that a negotiated peace was the best means of preventing Marshal's rebellion from turning into a general civil war. At the same time, Henry III thought it wise to forgive Llywelyn his attack earlier in the year by offering terms for a more lasting peace. Henry was keen to prevent Llywelyn from joining Marshal and as evidence of his good faith, the king granted Dafydd the manor of Purleigh in Essex. The gift was accepted but no peace was concluded, only an extension of the truce Llywelyn had renewed annually with the Crown since 1231. Llywelyn was biding his time and awaiting the results of the quarrel between the king and Marshal. He realised that this had the potential to be as divisive a conflict as the one that marred the last years of John's reign. When Marshal broke off negotiations with the king and returned to the offensive, Llywelyn came off his fence and sided with the baronial opposition. According to the native chroniclers, 'the earl made a solemn pact and agreement with the Lord Llywelyn and with the Welsh', and together they 'gathered an exceeding numerous host' and went on the offensive, attacking, besieging and burning nearly a dozen castles ranging from Cardiff and Abergavenny in the east to Carmarthen in the west.[51]

In a highly mobile and successful campaign, the king's forces were humiliated in a skirmish at Grosmont and defeated in a pitched battle near Monmouth. Llywelyn assisted in Marshal's conquest of the Earldom of Glamorgan while the latter supported the prince's retention of Cardigan. However, the allies did not enjoy success everywhere. The princelings of Deheubarth, Rhys Gryg, Owain ap Gruffudd, and Maelgwn Fychan, failed in their attempt to take Carmarthen castle in spite of a three-month siege. Worse still, a naval force under the command of Henry Turberville, lord of Crughywel, scattered and slaughtered the Welsh forces. Among those mortally wounded was the old warhorse, Rhys Gryg, who died shortly afterwards and was buried near his father, the Lord Rhys, in St David's Cathedral. Early in 1234, Marshal left to continue the rebellion in Ireland, but misfortune befell him when he was betrayed and killed by those who professed to be his allies. Hearing the news, Llywelyn may have thought the time ripe to make peace with the Crown and in March, at Brocton in Shropshire, a truce was agreed. This was followed in June by the sealing of the Pact of Myddle. Thereafter, Llywelyn's supremacy in native Wales remained unchallenged until his death six years later.

Notes

[1] *AWR.*, 398.
[2] Giles, *Roger of Wendover*, II, 119.
[3] Carpenter, D.A., *The Reign of Henry III* (London, 1996), 45.
[4] Walker, R.F., 'Hubert de Burgh and Wales, 1218-32', *English History Review*, 87 (1972), 467.
[5] *BT.Pen.*, 95.
[6] *Ibid.*, 96.
[7] *Ibid.*, 96.
[8] Carr, *NewDNB*, online edn.
[9] Smith, *Llywelyn ap Gruffudd*, 22.
[10] *Ibid.*, 22.
[11] *BT.Pen.*, 96.
[12] Lloyd, *HW*, II, 655.
[13] *AWR.*, 408.
[14] *BT.RBH.*, 221.
[15] *BT.Pen.*, 98.
[16] *Ibid.*
[17] *Ibid.*
[18] *Ibid.*
[19] *Ibid.*, 99.
[20] Walker, 'Hubert de Burgh and Wales', *EHR.*, 474.
[21] *BT.Pen.*, 100.
[22] Walker, 'Hubert de Burgh and Wales', *EHR.*, 473.
[23] *AWR.*, 417.
[24] Pryce, Huw, 'Negotiating Anglo-Welsh Relations: Llywelyn the Great and Henry III', in Weiler, Björn K.U.; Rowlands, Ifor W. (eds.), *England and Europe in the Reign of Henry III (1216-1272)* (Aldershot, 2002), 18.
[25] *AWR.*, 417.
[26] Lloyd, *HW*, II, 664.
[27] Walker, 'Hubert de Burgh and Wales', *EHR.*, 479.
[28] *Ibid.*, 480.
[29] *BT.Pen.*, 101.
[30] *Ibid.*
[31] Quoted in Walker, 'Hubert de Burgh and Wales', *EHR.*, 476.
[32] Lloyd, *HW*, II, 669.

[33] *BT.Pen.*, 102.
[34] *Calendar of Ancient Correspondence concerning Wales.* Edited by J.G. Edwards (Cardiff, 1935), 37.
[35] Lloyd, *HW*, II, 670.
[36] Maund, *The Welsh Kings*, 124.
[37] Pryce, 'Negotiating Anglo-Welsh Relations', 13.
[38] *AWR.*, 428.
[39] *Ibid.*, 429
[40] *Ibid.*, 428.
[41] *Ibid.*, 429.
[42] *Calendar of Close Rolls, 1227-31*, 368.
[43] Lloyd, *HW*, II, 672.
[44] *CAC.*, 35.
[45] *Ibid.*, 53.
[46] *BT.Pen.*, 102.
[47] Quoted in Walker, 'Hubert de Burgh and Wales', *EHR.*, 490.
[48] Quoted in Carpenter, *Britain 1066-1284*, 314.
[49] *BT.Pen.*, 102.
[50] *Ibid.*, 102.
[51] *Ibid.*, 103.

VI

Politics, Power and Propaganda:
'Prince of Aberffraw, Lord of Snowdon'.

> The Archdeacon marvelled greatly that the King had
> already got knowledge of the affair, and also that any
> man should have reached the King sooner than himself,
> who had travelled at great speed, unless indeed it be
> that, since rumour does in truth fly on wings to kings
> and princes, from whom scarce anything may be hid,
> notable events are ever quick to reach them.[1]
>
> [*The Autobiography of Gerald of Wales*]

The prince stood at the heart of developments in war, politics,
government and their administration; each was conducted in his
name and each was effected by means of his authority. Successful
rulers were those able to convert this authority into power and
among the first of the princes to do this successfully in Wales was
Llywelyn ap Iorwerth. He maintained himself in power by a
combination of military skill and political dexterity. He had
seized every opportunity to extend the limits of his rule, while at
the same time carefully watching the temper of English kings –
Richard, John and Henry III – and guarding himself from any
step that might permanently alienate him or them. Under his
powerful protection government, literature, law and religion
were able to evolve and prosper unfettered by outside
interference.

LLYWELYN THE WAR LORD: THE *TEULU* AND *LLU*

It is as a lord of men that we first encounter Llywelyn, and the
chief attributes of his lordship – leadership and dependence –
manifest themselves most clearly in war. Prince in name but
warlord by nature, Llywelyn, like many young noblemen of his

time, roamed the land almost at will with their warrior companions, plundering, 'ravaging' and causing mayhem as they went. He did this in the name of honour and in the cause of glory, and, as befitting a heroic society, in search of a reputation. Laden with spoil, the prince would reward his faithful followers and, in so doing, establish the means of controlling them. These dependants became the prince's key supporters, a ruling elite bound to a common overlord by ties of service and comradeship in arms.

Indeed, if the poets are to be believed, it was primarily by means of military lordship as distinct from land-lordship and economic lordship that Llywelyn ruled so that terror more than territory formed the basis of his authority. It is impossible to assess the merits or otherwise of the fighting skills of individual princes since the evidence does not permit such detailed pictures to be drawn, but whether they were all as successful or as great as the native literati would have us believe is another matter. True to the eulogistic tradition of contemporary native prose, the poets and chroniclers magnified and exaggerated their patrons' personal contribution to the success of battles. This serves to illustrate the crucial role played by Llywelyn as a commander and strategist rather than simply as a participating warrior. He was keenly aware that his power, perhaps his very survival, relied on military might which, in turn, depended as much on his own personal courage and prowess as a warrior as on his ability to inspire and command others.

Praise was one thing, reward another, and if war was the source of honour and glory it was also the source of plunder and profit. Thus in 1233 could the *Brut* equate Llywelyn's success in carrying 'many spoils away' from his enemies with returning 'home eminently worthy'.[2] However, whereas the princes of old were essentially conquerors of men and not territory, this was not the case by the time Llywelyn had begun his campaign to make himself master of Gwynedd. By the beginning of the thirteenth century, there was a subtle but discernible shift in the attitude of the native literati towards their rulers who came to be regarded not so much as all-conquering war-leaders but as protectors, peace-makers and law-enforcers. Increasingly, native rulers were coming to be judged as politicians, diplomats, justices and administrators; hence the praise heaped on Llywelyn by the poet Dafydd Benfras for being 'our common ruler' and a 'gentle advocate in the council of the wise'.[3]

Nevertheless, it must not be thought that taking on the mantle of civilian government in any way diminished their accustomed role as the military leaders. Indeed, irrespective of the developing political and bureaucratic sophistication of the princes, the exercise of real power never moved far beyond their ability to field an effective fighting force and to fund the construction of castles. At the heart of this 'fighting force', was the *teulu*, the core element that made it effective and the hub around which Welsh military life revolved. A body of well-trained professional troops pledged to protect their prince, the royal retinue was regarded in Welsh law as one of the three indispensable necessities of royal status (the others being his priest and court justice).

Yet times were changing and Llywelyn was one of those princes with vision enough to realize that in order to establish a viable state he needed the support of a force more substantial than a war band; he needed an army, commensurate with the ambitions of his statecraft. The Welsh laws make clear that the military forces available to the prince were made up of more than just his warrior nobility; they consisted of his subjects entire. This was the general military levy, the army, which the native chroniclers tend to refer to as the host or *llu* as opposed to the *teulu* or war-band. The *llu* catered only for those freemen – the majority – who did not serve as part of the *teulu*. Trained though they were in arms, their entitlement to land enabled them to take up its cultivation and management so that they 'passed into the general body of tribesmen'[4] who could be called on to serve their prince in war only according to fixed rules. Within the bounds of his kingdom, the prince could call on all freemen to serve him at will and should any be incapable of bearing arms, the onus was on the incapacitated to provide able-bodied men in their stead. In stark contrast, Llywelyn's right to raise troops for service beyond those territories that constituted his domain was limited to once a year and for a period not exceeding six weeks.

As the twin demands of war and defence, allied to ever greater political ambition, impacted on the prince, he was forced to widen his recruitment base, which in turn enabled him to field larger and more professionally organised armies. Inevitably, this impacted also on tactics and the methods employed in meeting the enemy in the field, particularly in open combat. Increasingly, it was the size of the princely *llu*, rather than the *teulu*, which came to reflect Llywelyn's growing power, importance and ambition. This is confirmed to some extent by the chronicles, which significantly make no mention of his *teulu*, or that of any prince, after 1215. This is not to say that the *teulu* as a military institution disappeared or even declined in importance, but merely to suggest that its role may have changed from being the principal offensive weapon of the prince into a body more concerned with his defence and personal protection.

Yet if war enabled Llywelyn to demonstrate his military prowess and enhance his reputation, it contributed little to the effective government of his own realm. War was an expensive business, the spiralling costs of which threatened to outstrip his resources. The prince had to find the means to raise, fund and equip an army rather than a retinue. A large army notwithstanding, it was in the competitive area of new technology linked to castle-building that Llywelyn had to make his mark. The transition from wooden to stone castles is a tangible expression of the consolidation of a prince's power. However, in seeking a permanent and visible symbol of his authority by means of a network of stone castles, Llywelyn required not just new sources of continuing funding but the administration to effect their construction, maintenance and garrison.

THE CASTLE

If the war-band or *teulu* in particular, and the army or *llu* in general, were primarily the instrument of conquest, then the castle may be regarded as the primary instrument of

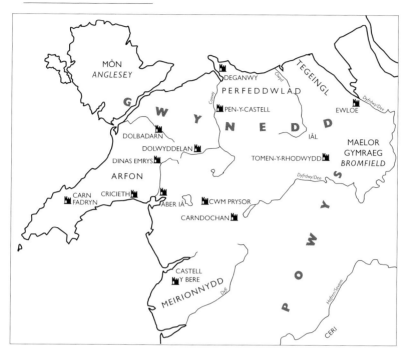

The Castles of Gwynedd.

consolidation. Military lordship was most clearly represented by the castle because it symbolised lordship just as it consolidated lordship. Llywelyn showed that he was as concerned as his Anglo-Norman neighbours to erect castles with the express purpose of controlling land for either strategic, administrative or political reasons. It is the equation between disposable income and masonry construction and military/political imperatives that is critical. In order to survive, the prince had to compete with his rivals, which required him to bend his resources towards masonry construction on a massive scale using the latest technology.

As early as 1188, Gerald of Wales noted on his tour of Gwynedd that 'two stone castles have been built there recently' – Aber Ia near Porthmadog and Carn Fadryn in the Llŷn peninsula – which may suggest a conscious imitation on the part of the northern princes of the systematic building programme and strategic policies followed by the Lord Rhys in the south.

Although these two early stone castles appear to have been simply built of unmortared masonry, they were but the first of some fifteen stone castles of ever-increasing size and sophistication, both in terms of the quality of the materials used and the methods of construction adopted, erected by the princes of Gwynedd in the century between 1180 and 1280.

The prince thought to be responsible for erecting all but five of these fifteen fortresses was Llywelyn ap Iorwerth. Though not the first to erect native castles, Llywelyn was foremost among the more powerful princes to grasp the wider strategic significance of castle-building, in pursuit of political as well as military objectives as opposed to narrower tactical advantages. It has been demonstrated by Glanville Jones that by taking account of the location and structural sophistication of Llywelyn's castles, it is possible to reconstruct a coherent picture of the military aspect of his state-building activities in the first half of the thirteenth century. The disposition of Llywelyn's castles suggests that they were sited with deliberation perhaps partly, as Glanville Jones argues, 'to establish control over a barrier zone to the south and east so as to protect the Venedotian heartland in Arfon, Llŷn and Anglesey',[5] but certainly, as A.D. Carr suggests, 'to cover internal lines of communication and as a defence against an external enemy.'[6] Unlike in Deheubarth under the Lord Rhys, Llywelyn did not establish a stone castle in each of the thirteen lordships or *cantrefi* that made up his domain; his castles were built for military and strategic reasons with no apparent thought to supplant the traditional commotal *llys* (local court) as an administrative centre. Indeed, a number of the more impressive commotal *llysoedd* continued to function, no doubt fortified for the purpose, alongside the castles as occasional residences for the itinerant royal family, Aberffraw and Aber near Bangor prominent among them.

The efficacy of Llywelyn's castle-building programme and its strategic importance for Gwynedd are testified by the fact that his successors, his son Dafydd and more particularly his grandson Llywelyn ap Gruffudd, sought to strengthen, rather than to supplement or replace, the existing strongholds. The castles of

Photograph of Dolbadarn Castle.   *(Cadw, Crown copyright)*

Cricieth, Carndochan, Deganwy, Dolbadarn, Dolwyddelan, Ewloe and Y Bere exhibit signs of having been refurbished, some to a considerable degree. Clearly, these castles had become pivotal points in the defence of Gwynedd and in the maintenance of order within the principality.

If, as has been suggested, this use of finely sculpted, decorated stonework in at least two of the castles attributed to Llywelyn – at Castell y Bere and Deganwy where the carved stone head found at the site is thought to represent the prince – is tantamount to demonstrating his 'concern with a conspicuous display of status',[7] then it suggests that beyond their domestic and military use these castles had a higher purpose: they were symbols of the princes' authority designed as much to overawe their subjects as to impress their visitors, hostile or otherwise. The symbolism of power was very important to the princes who appear intent on embedding some of their most strategically valuable fortresses in the culture and mythology of their Celtic past. Built away from traditional sites, commotal *llysoedd* or places of especial cultural significance, these castles were erected for their strategic importance alone. It has been demonstrated that of the castles built in Gwynedd by the Llywelyns, only one, Deganwy, a traditional site dating back to the post-Roman period, was located at the commotal *llys*.

We should not, therefore, discount the importance of symbolism as a factor in their construction and certainly not regard the castle as an 'optional extra'. In fact, the castle was quickly absorbed into the militaristic culture of the Welsh warrior elite, so much so that a new clause was added to the native law-texts specifying that everyone, with few exceptions, was required to undertake castle-building duties for the ruler. There were other changes too, not least in the methods of warfare, for the Welsh had to adapt to new technology, in terms not only of castle construction but of castle destruction, and new techniques of siege warfare. This called for a radical re-think on the part of the Welsh but they were not found wanting. By the 1230s, Llywelyn had acquired more sophisticated siege equipment with which to take castles, such as the 'catapults' he deployed to take the castle of Cardigan in 1231.[8]

Although personal bravery on the battlefield continued to find favour with the literati, songsters and poets, and no doubt did no small service in greatly augmenting the prestige of a prince, it was to be his skill as a strategist and tactician, as a besieger of castles and commander of armies in the field, that would ultimately contribute to his political success, which, by itself, had probably become the only sure means of safeguarding a Welsh ruler's survival and the survival of his kingdom.

GOVERNMENT AND RULERSHIP

If the early princes did not govern in the bureaucratic sense of the word, they certainly ruled and they did so over a subject people, the majority of whom served them less according to their 'office' and more on account of their class or status in society. In the traditional schema of the three orders, it was generally, if simplistically, accepted that freemen fought, clerics taught but villeins wrought. Irrespective of their class or status, the focus for all was the royal court or *llys* which was established in every district and at which they rendered their submissions, paid their dues and performed their services.

As befitting the personal nature of their rule, it was here that the princes might meet their subjects as they went on progress through their lands. The importance of this aspect of princely rule is underlined by the anonymous biographer of Llywelyn's great-grandfather, Gruffudd ap Cynan, who stated that having recovered Gwynedd from his enemies, the prince was encouraged 'to go on circuit around his patrimony' so that he might 'subdue Anglesey and Arfon and Llŷn and the cantrefs bordering England' by taking 'homage (*gwrogaeth*) from their people' (*gwerin*).[9] Llywelyn's consolidation and defence of his authority in his dominions rested upon his mastery of the art of warfare and this in turn rested upon his ability to turn his capital resources into available wealth. His technique for enhancing his prosperity was not due simply to conquest and plunder but also to efficient management of his domain: in short, more intensive and regular lordship.

Since the native princes are not known to have minted their own coin, the ultimate source of most of the money circulating in Wales must have been England. On the other hand, there is a report from Edward Lhuyd, dated June 1698, that one of the relations of the Bishop of Bangor had kept 'in his Pocket several Years' a coin issued by Llywelyn, which he 'shewed . . . to many of the Bishops Acquantance, still living, who confirm it.'[10] The gradual adoption of a moneyed economy in Gwynedd may have been facilitated in part by Llywelyn's close relations with the English court and Marcher lords. That he was able to found and patronize religious houses across north Wales presupposes the existence of surplus wealth. It is instructive that when Llywelyn wished to bind the burgesses of Brecon to an agreement, it was in terms of coin, to the tune of a hundred marks, rather than kind that he did so. The prince's growing dependence on cash revenues and monetary transactions is well illustrated by the growth of commutation in Gwynedd during the thirteenth century. Traditional renders, dues and services were systematically commuted into cash payments and their collection more tightly organized in order to meet the spiralling costs of government and war. Cash payments aside, the prince's subjects were still expected to render dues and services that included time-honoured obligations by the freemen to provide accommodation for the king's officers when touring the local courts. Exploitation of the prince's demesne lands, which were to be found in every commote usually close to the *llys*, was systematised and regularised, commercial activity was encouraged, tolls and customs duties were levied and even a form of extraordinary taxation imposed.

If the twelfth century witnessed a great increase in the nature and scope of administrative activity, it is in the thirteenth that we encounter the trappings of bureaucratic government. True there was little in the way of administrative specialisation, and institutions like the prince's council were not fully developed, but the fact that historians can speak in terms of a 'ministerial elite' serving the princes of Gwynedd, sporting familiar titles such as steward, chancellor, justiciar, chamberlain and treasurer, suggests that there were powerful forces at work making for change. The catalysts for change were the princes themselves since it was largely their ambition, drive and energy, for power, wealth and territory, which stimulated those around them into seeking new ways to best serve them. Consciously, and sometimes unconsciously, the princes and their 'ministers' imitated, copied and borrowed from their neighbours, the Crown and the Anglo–Norman Marcher lords, so that theirs was a bureaucratic hybrid composed of several layers extending from the centre almost web-like into the localities. Of course, to contemporaries, government must have seemed almost entirely a local affair and so it was and largely remained so, but during Llywelyn's reign there was a discernible shift towards concentrating the business of government in the hands of those at the centre. Where that centre was depended very much on the location of the prince around whom government was fashioned and in whom power was concentrated.

AGENTS OF PRINCELY GOVERNMENT

Economic lordship had implications for other aspects of lordship and there were limits as to how far a ruler could press his subjects, particularly those on whom he relied to govern. If neither the will nor consent of the people at large was considered a prerequisite for realising the potential of 'good lordship', it was essential that he have it of his 'leading men'. A descriptive term that recurs regularly in contemporary texts, 'leading men' were those that probably had a significant impact on princely government and in its development. These were the men with whom the princes hunted and generally consorted, in whom they trusted, of whom in war they boasted and on whom they relied for counsel.

That their counsel was heeded is much in evidence in the native chronicles which offer tantalising glimpses of their work and worth. For example, it was, according to Gerald of Wales, 'by the advice of his good counsellors'[11] that Llywelyn invested his kinsmen with land in Gwynedd. Who these 'good' men were is not generally known but chief among those whose names have come down to us was Ednyfed Fychan, a soldier and administrator of special talent. Ednyfed Fychan succeeded Gwyn ab Ednywain as Llywelyn's *distain* or seneschal, sometime between 1215 and 1217 when he first appears as a witness in connection with the prince's grant to Morgan Gam of land in Gower. Thereafter, according to J.E. Lloyd, 'he is constantly engaged in the business of the prince, and it cannot be doubted that the part he played in shaping the policy of Gwynedd was substantial.'[12] Certainly as *distain* of Gwynedd, Ednyfed was, to all intents and purposes, the prince's leading judge, chief financial agent and chief executive officer.

The 'leading men' of Gwynedd could exert considerable influence on their prince perhaps even to the point of compelling him to act contrary to his will. This is what Llywelyn found when, in 1211, 'by the counsel of his leading men', he was advised 'to seek to make peace with the king on whatever terms he could.'[13] Unfortunately for them, one of the conditions imposed by King John was that Llywelyn give him 'hostages from amongst the leading men of the land.'[14] Nevertheless, it is equally clear that ultimately power rested in the prince and though his counsellors could advise, forcefully at times, they might not be permitted to decide or dictate policy.

THE PRINCE'S COUNCIL

At what point counsellors became councillors is not easy to determine, but that they did so is indicative of the gradual institutionalisation of significant aspects of princely government and administration. Although it is not until the early years of the thirteenth century that we have anything like a reliable reference to what appears to have been a properly constituted princely council, it is reasonable to assume that there had existed a council of sorts for some time before this. On a purely practical level the princes could hardly consult all their nobility on a regular basis and for the sake of efficient government a core element, the so-called 'leading men', might be called upon to serve in council. This is hinted at in a communication of Llywelyn's to King Philip of France in 1212 in which reference is made to a 'council of my chieftains' when ratifying a treaty of alliance between the Welsh prince and the French king.[15]

Thereafter, the councils of the princes of Gwynedd are much more in evidence and it is perhaps a measure of their importance that reference to them is usually in connection with great matters of state such as wars, treaties, alliances and settling disputes particularly between his 'leading men'. Nevertheless, it was the personality and will of the prince that dominated Gwynedd and what mattered was not so much Llywelyn's 'right' or 'power' to act independently of his council, but the way in which he exercised those rights and effected his powers. In short, the sucessful prince was one who tempered his masterfulness with concessions.

How far the council was a legislative and executive body, if such terms can be applied let alone be distinguished, cannot now be properly assessed since our knowledge of princely administration is incomplete. Nevertheless, it may not be too far short of the truth to suggest that although the council's primary duty was, and remained, to proffer advice and act as a sounding board, in some instances, such as in matters of jurisprudence, it did involve itself in what appears to have approximated to a 'legislative' process. In a judicial inquiry convened by Edward I in 1281 to investigate the operation and jursidiction of Welsh law, depositions were taken from various witnesses, both English and Welsh, which shed light not only on the role of the council in the making and amending of law but, more significantly, on that of the princes also. The fact that Llywelyn and his grandson and namesake were thought by some deponents to have often disregarded native law in favour of English legal procedure suggests that the matter of the law, its administration and its development, lay very much at the prince's will.

Their arrogation of legislative power in matters of law and justice notwithstanding, the princes may not have been entirely free to act (or might have thought it imprudent to do so) without consulting their nobility, particularly, but perhaps not exclusively, those in council. Having the authority to 'reform' the law with the 'assent' of his nobility, it is perhaps only natural to find the prince working closely with them, particularly those sitting in council. Indeed, it is in terms of its judicial work that the council comes closest to fulfilling what might be called an 'executive' role when it sat, along with the prince, in judgement on the latter's subjects. The council was more than 'a mere cypher'.[16]

Clearly, the prince needed the advice and support of his nobility and, where applicable, he shared his lordship with them, but the successful prince was the one who managed at the same time to maintain his authority over them.

LAW MAKING AND LAW REFORM

The prince represented the highest form of justice and, as a dispenser of justice, he had the power to institute changes in the law. Although the main body of native law was based on custom rather than on princely legislation, by the beginning of the thirteenth century (if not earlier), the princes had, for want of a better term, 'acquired' the power not only to 'amend', 'correct', 'amplify' and 'abbreviate' the laws but also to 'grant' and 'abolish' them. Nor can we rule out entirely the possibility, as expressed by Huw Pryce, 'that custom had itself been shaped in part by princely legislation, which may also have left its mark on some of the legal rules.'[17]

It is widely acknowledged that Llywelyn, like Rhys ap Gruffudd of Deheubarth before him, was responsible for some reform of native law. The so-called Venedotian Code was a northern edition of the laws of Hywel Dda compiled by Iorwerth ap Madog about the beginning of the thirteenth century. The fact that this lawbook was compiled at all suggests that there was some juristic activity in Llywelyn's court. However, the nature of the changes effected by Llywelyn are not properly defined though it seems they were directed towards a greater insistence on royal rights. His letter to Pope Honorious III in 1222 certainly points to some judicial activity on the part of the prince in that he was prepared to abolish 'detestable' customs that were 'contrary to divine and human law'.[18]

Given his attempts to establish a wider hegemony, the territorial division of Deheubarth at Aberdyfi in 1216 and the dispossessions of Elise ap Madog of Penllyn in 1202 and of Maredudd ap Madog in 1238 suggest that legal precedents were being set by him in his treatment of his fellow princes. In the opinion of Rees Davies,

> This association of prince and law was particularly clear in Gwynedd, for there Welsh law was consciously employed not only to promote princely power in general but also to further Gwynedd's claim to the political leadership of native Wales.[19]

Llywelyn was among the more astute and sensitive of Welsh rulers who realised that the law, both native and the borrowings from Angevin and later 'English' law, must be taken in hand and fashioned to the needs of the state, thereby becoming an indispensable tool of government. Not that there was much to choose between them since, in truth, governing and law-keeping were not separate activities, which explains why the courts and councils of the princes, in common with those on the continent, had always exhibited a strong judicial aspect. By the making, amending and enforcing of law and the dispensing of justice, the princes were not only enhancing their status and prestige but adding materially to their wealth and power.

The profits of justice came to loom large in princely incomes, a fact which helps to explain the concomitant expansion of their judicial competence. That the prince came to levy and collect fines from his subjects not only enabled him to augment his revenue but reinforced his position as the fount of law and justice. Gradually, but noticeably, the agencies of princely authority, the commotal courts and royal officers, assumed a greater role in the dispensing of justice which in turn contributed to the growth of the concept of public order. Thus could the poet Llywarch ap Llywelyn sing that 'Tonight, wherever you look there is peace'.[20]

Although Llywelyn cannot lay claim to a Welsh version of the title accorded Edward I, 'The English Justinian', for 'the importance and permanence of his legislation and the dignity of his position in legal history',[21] he was, nonetheless, more than a mere mechanic; rather an engineer who sought not only to bend and shape the law to his own use but to 'correct' the law for the common good.

THE ROYAL COURT

The hub around which princely governance revolved was the court. Here would be found the prince's domestic servants, military retainers, courtiers and clerics, some of whom served as one of the twenty-four officers of the court. Largely domestic in origin and function, the elaborate hierarchy of court officials depicted in the lawbooks was seriously out of step with the reality of developments in the latter half of the twelfth and in the thirteenth century. By this time the more significant of the court officers in Gwynedd, namely the steward (*distain*), chamberlain (*gwas ystafell*), possibly the court judge (*ynad llys*) and perhaps even the household priest (*offeiriad teulu*), had evolved sufficiently to take a more active role in government, which had itself become a more complex administrative operation. At its heart was the council which, as we have seen, came to assume a more formal role under the princes of Gwynedd and at its head was the steward (*senescallus*) who became the prince's chief governmental officer and principal advisor. It is evident from the lawbooks and other contemporary sources that he had the authority to dispense justice; hence the frequency with which he is termed justiciar (*justiciarius*) with the power to act in the prince's absence, one of three officers so empowered, and with the right to lead troops in war.

Yet Rees Davies has affirmed his belief that 'None of the courts of the native Welsh rulers developed the specialisation of function which was coming to characterise the *curia regis* in England.'[22] Certainly, the princes had a writing office, a 'great' and 'privy' or 'secret' seal to authenticate the ever-increasing volume of charters and letters, the means to keep track of its records and a staff of clerks to see to its running. The general consensus of opinion favours the existence of a loosely organised secretariat staffed by a number of clerks, any one of whom was capable of drawing up and issuing the prince's charters and letters. That said, it is likely that the chancellor alone of the secretariat had access to, and possibly the keeping of, the great seal and it is to him that the prince's diplomata were brought for sealing. In one instance, the absence of his chancellor may have caused Llywelyn some embarrassment in that he had to explain that he was 'sealing the letters with his secret seal, because he has not his great seal with him.'[23] Although the charters and writs that expressed the prince's will and pleasure must have originated in the *curia*, it has been suggested that much of the work of a 'chancery' may well have been done elsewhere, most probably in the religious houses dotted around Gwynedd but principally the Cistercian abbeys of Aberconwy and Cymer. Their skills in writing, copying and record keeping made these houses ideally suited for the tasks required of a 'chancery'. Moreover, their loyalty to Llywelyn, a generous benefactor, earned them the trust and patronage of their royal master.

This does not mean that the princes of Gwynedd had departed entirely from the system of administration that operated by delegating royal authority to prominent landholders in the localities in which they dwelt. However, these were men not easily removed and although it was hoped to bind them into a closer, and mutually beneficial, union, it was not always possible to trust them. Indeed, if the evidence from Gwynedd is typical, it seems that the princes tended to rely on the service of a small group of powerful families, perhaps no more than half a dozen in north Wales, which suggests that there was little scope for reward or largesse for those outside this inner circle. This may have been due to a lack of material resources or else a deliberate policy for the better management of a restricted circle of servants.

Llywelyn's achievement was not that he created a large dominion but that he introduced to it the art of government. There can be no government without the control of men, and without a regular standing army, other than the *teulu*, that control came by means of the church and social bonds – in other words, kindred groups and local community chains of obligation. By overlaying these with a network of lordship and vassalage, the prince was attempting to institutionalise his 'office' and thereby become the most important element in the government of the realm. Apart from the prince himself, there were two main foci of power: the administration, centring on the council, and the royal household or court. Both were gradually institutionalised and territorialised so that a prince's power and authority were widened and made real to those whom the ruler employed and professed to govern.

TOWARDS A PRINCIPALITY OF WALES

The foundations of a greater Venedotian state were laid by Llywelyn at Aberdyfi in 1216, when he largely succeeded in binding the other lords and princes of Wales by ties of clientship and dependence which involved the swearing of oaths of fealty.

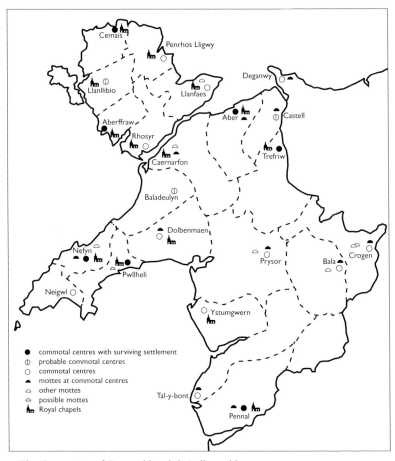

The Commotes of Gwynedd and their *llysoedd*.

Llywelyn's achievement was lauded by the poet Dafydd Benfras, who hailed his patron as 'the great chieftain of fair Wales' and 'the ruler of rulers'.[24] Llywelyn's pre-eminence was to endure for the rest of his life and although he suffered the odd setback, most notably the loss of Carmarthen and Cardigan in 1223 and his submission to the king at Montgomery in 1228, he continued to dominate Wales and Welsh affairs. That he wished to convert vague notions of overlordship into something more tangible and permanent is made clear from his subsequent claims and actions.

As early as 1220, Llywelyn attempted to territorialise and make real his claims to lordship beyond his patrimony when he defended the rights of Cadwallon and Maredudd, sons of Maelgwn ap Cadwallon, to rule in the lordship in Maelienydd. Pressed by the king to hand the lordship over to the Mortimer family, the prince demurred, claiming that 'the homage of these men belongs to Llywelyn's principality.'[25] This is the earliest known use of the term *principatum*, which J. Beverley Smith is convinced was designed to 'convey the idea of a broad political entity under the supremacy of Aberffraw.'[26] In 1226 Llywelyn strengthened his right to exercise his overlordship beyond Gwynedd by granting southern Powys to his son Gruffudd. This was followed, in 1230, by his adoption of the title Prince of Aberffraw and Lord of Snowdon, which, according to Huw Pryce, 'proclaimed his dual status as both overlord of the whole of native Wales and ruler of his patrimonial principality of Gwynedd.'[27]

In order to fulfil his ambition Llywelyn would need to claim the homages of the other Welsh lords and princes, but his attempt to do so in 1238 was blocked by the Crown. Aware of the implications of giving up or transferring its right to the homage of the Welsh princes, the Crown never offered Llywelyn the comprehensive peace treaty he sought, nor did it confirm his territorial gains. Although Llywelyn's authority over his dependents was, in the opinion of Rees Davies, 'extensive and interventionist', he believes the prince 'made no attempt to forge this augmented native Wales into a single kingdom.'[28] Indeed, he maintained that Llywelyn's power and authority was 'patriarchal rather than institutional', and that his aim was 'to create a federation under his presidency rather than to amalgamate the various principalities and regions into a single unit.'[29] M.T. Clanchy agrees stating that 'Llywelyn was not a king and feudal overlord but a prince in the sense of principal ruler.'[30] There is a great deal of truth in this but the conscious adoption of a new title culminating in the aims expressed in the council at Strata Florida suggests that something greater and more substantial was in preparation during the 1230s.

Llywelyn had no legal or customary precedent to follow but he knew that if his wider hegemony was to survive his death, he would need to forge anew, within some form of institutional framework, the ties that bound the other lords and princes to him and to his heir. 'There was therefore', according to A.D. Carr, 'a need to devise an entirely new body of law to govern the prince's relations with other rulers.'[31] It must not be forgotten that these 'other rulers' were themselves princes, or of princely descent, who, less than a century earlier, would have considered themselves, and been seen by others, as the equal of Llywelyn but who were now faced with the prospect of being reduced in status to his barons or tenants-in-chief. That Maredudd ap Madog of Powys Fadog was deprived of his patrimony for killing his brother points not only to the growing territorial jurisdiction of Llywelyn, his court and his justice, but to the recognition by others of that fact.

Unfortunately for Llywelyn, time ran out and he died before he was able to establish the legal and institutional framework necessary to ensure the survival of his wider hegemony. It was left to his grandson, Llywelyn ap Gruffudd, to attempt to institutionalise his position as prince of Wales, conceptualise the notion of the state and constitutionalise the relationship between himself and his clients and dependents.

LLYWELYN AND THE CHURCH

If the castle represented the chief monumental prop to the military and political power of the princes the church lagged not far behind. The prince was as active in founding and in constructing ecclesiastical structures as he was in building castles. The one built out of necessity; he had no choice because his very survival depended upon it. The other he built out of piety in the desperate hope that his charity and penance might secure for him a place in the after-life. Piety and necessity aside, the act and fact of building were as important as the structures themselves for in erecting churches, monasteries, palaces and castles, Llywelyn was underlining his hegemony, both real and symbolic, and thereby considerably enhancing his prestige.

Llywelyn may be described, in a phrase beloved of historians, as conventionally pious. If this is taken to mean that he was no better nor worse than the majority of his contemporaries, then it is apt. Unlike Louis VII of France, no contemporary ruling prince of Wales could be described as being so pious that 'you would think he was not a king but a man of religion.'[32] Nor could any Welsh prince rival the extravagant claim made on Louis's behalf by contemporary French chroniclers of his being 'the most christian of all princes.'[33] On the other hand, unlike King John, Llywelyn was never charged with irreligion, though he was temporarily excommunicated, nor did he earn the epithet ascribed to Henry II by Gerald of Wales, 'the hammer of the church.'[34]

It is perhaps to be expected that those on the point of death would almost inevitably turn to the Church for succour and comfort even after a life of cruelty and debauchery. Increasingly, remorse-racked princes turned to the nearest or most highly regarded monastic community and donned the clerical habit of their favoured order among whom they spent their final days or hours. Llywelyn was no exception, for as the *Brut* makes clear:

> the Lord Llywelyn ap Iorwerth ab Owain Gwynedd, prince of Wales . . . died after he had assumed the habit of the Order at Aberconwy; and he was buried honourably there.[35]

The Church was more than just an institution intended to care for the spiritual welfare of its flock; it was a powerful organisation with as much temporal, especially political, as spiritual influence and authority. If the secular world increasingly intruded into the spiritual domain so did the Church involve itself in the world beyond the cloister. Where possible Llywelyn sought to enlist the goodwill and co-operation of his leading clerics on whom he came to rely for service as bureaucrats, diplomats and technocrats. They were men of considerable wealth and territorial influence, learned and often well-connected; in short, probably the most important cogs in the machinery of princely government.

Yet their relationship with the Church in Wales was complicated as much by the role of Canterbury as by the influence of change. The one stemmed from the desire on the part of successive archbishops of Canterbury, fully supported by the English Crown, to subjugate Wales and assume the spiritual overlordship of the native bishoprics, and the other from the evolutionary pressures associated with what may be termed the 'religious renaissance' of the eleventh and twelfth centuries. It was a challenge which some of the more devout, or devious, princes met with considerable flair and imagination. According to Gerald of Wales, Llywelyn's influence was decisive in securing the election, in 1215, of Cadwgan, abbot of Whitland, to the bishopric of Bangor and, more significantly, of Iorwerth, abbot of Talley, to the diocese of St David's. He may also have been responsible for the election of Hywel ap Ednyfed to the see of St Asaph in 1240.

Unfortunately for Gerald, Llywelyn was unable to secure his election to the see of St David's. Twice, in 1176 and 1198, Gerald attempted to win the see for himself but he was thwarted on both occasions by king and archbishop. Gerald's enemies were aware of his aim to enhance the status of St David's by securing papal recognition of its metropolitan authority. Had Gerald succeeded, the Welsh Church might have gained independence from Canterbury and he become its first archbishop. Llywelyn fully appreciated the significance of Gerald's campaign both for his own political ambition and for a Welsh Church unfettered by English authority. The prince supported Gerald whom he met to discuss the issue in 1202. Indeed, Llywelyn issued a letter patent to the St David's Cathedral Chapter, which had elected Gerald bishop against the wishes of the Crown, in this he promised that

> If any of the canons or clerks of the church of St. David's should lose anything on account of their supporting Archdeacon Gerald, Llywelyn would provide twofold restitution; he would also receive honourably and generously in his own land any that were driven into exile for that reason.[36]

Llywelyn was not shy of using his patronage of, and close association with, the Church as an additional tool of government.

For example, to help quell opposition and punish the recalcitrant, Llywelyn could seek excommunication and interdict with the acquiescence of compliant clerics. Thus were the lands of Madog ap Gruffudd Maelor laid under interdict sometime between 1215 and 1217 when he planned a marriage of which his overlord Llywelyn did not approve. On the other hand, such cynical use of the Church and its authority tended to rebound on those most active and opportunistic in its exploitation. Both Llywelyn and his grandson were themselves victims of the weapon of excommunication pronounced by English bishops at the behest of a king of England.

It was in the monastic sphere that Llywelyn showed himself to be the enlightened friend of reform. He patronised the Cistercians and issued charters confirming to the abbeys of Cymer and Aberconwy their extensive lands in north Wales. He welcomed the Franciscans and supported the Augustinians, but he may have done so at the expense of the native Church for in four instances Llywelyn transferred the ancient foundations of Aberdaron, Bardsey, Beddgelert and Penmon wholesale to the Augustinians. These transfers, endowments and foundations created a land-rich monastic community, which further enriched itself by its economic activities and trade. It has been estimated that within a quarter of a century of the foundation of Aberconwy in 1186 it had accumulated an estate of near 40,000 acres. Aside from the considerable economic and political benefits (and pitfalls), we need not doubt the sincerity of Llywelyn's motives in founding and patronizing religious houses, some of which became closely identified with members of his family, such as the priory of Llanfaes which served as his wife's mausoleum.

Clearly, princely patronage represented a significant element in the Church. Much of its wealth in land and its privileges in law were as a result of munificent endowments and generous exemptions by princes. Its bishops and abbots, some of whom owed their clerical office to the patronage of princes, were among the wealthiest and most powerful men in the country and much the best educated. In return for their patronage, the princes expected their leading clerics to serve them as advisors, administrators, ambassadors and mediators. At least thirteen clerics have been identified as being in the service of Llywelyn, these ranged in importance from bishops to clerks: the Bishops of Bangor included Robert (d.1212), Cadwgan (d.1236) and Richard (d.1267) and those of St Asaph were Reiner (d.1224), Abraham (d.1232) and Hywel (d.1240). The lesser clergy included David, Archdeacon of St. Asaph, Masters Adam and Philip ab Ifor, clerks Simon, David, John and most significant of all, given his length of service (1204-31), Instructus. In peace and war Llywelyn's most enduring support came from the church, which sustained his dynasty by shaping lay opinion through sermons and ritual. Liturgical processions, coronation ceremonial and, ultimately, its sanction of secular authority by men consecrated to their positions, all contributed to enhancing the prestige of an ambitious Prince of Gwynedd.

This is not to suggest that the relationship between prince and Church was without problems since there were tensions and pressures here too. Second only to the princes in terms of wealth and power, the Church dominated much of the public life, politics and culture of Wales. Naturally, the princes sought to control the Church and attempted to do so through a combination of patronage and coercion depending on the pliancy of the personnel or institutions involved. However, unlike his grandson and namesake, Llywelyn seems not to have encountered any opposition from the clerical community in Wales.

PRINCELY PATRONAGE

Patronage was as much a servant of politics as it was of the arts and religion, and Llywelyn was keenly aware of the power of patronage in augmenting his political authority. Patronage for priests and poets contributed as much to maintaining the social order through peace, law and justice as did the other agencies at the disposal of the ruler. Indeed, if adroit patronage was indispensable to successful rulership so, in equal measure, were piety and propaganda specifically tailored to the needs of the prince.

It is in his patronage of the select band of bards or court poets, the so-called *Beirdd y Tywysogyon* (literally, poets of the princes), that Llywelyn took a direct hand in the support and encouragement of Welsh culture. At the royal court of Aberffraw, the bards entertained and delighted their royal and noble audiences with their inventive and ingenious verse, which was almost exclusively sung or chanted to musical accompaniment, primarily the harp. As befitted the age, the warrior audience and the prevailing 'fashion' in poetic composition, much of the verse was panegyric and elegiac in content and style. Poetic renditions of heroic deeds and glorious battles, fine deaths and honourable victories were popular and very much in demand. Despite the formal and stylised nature of the poetry, there is no reason to dispute its ability to entertain the prince whose love for, and patronage of, the art was as much a product of habit as of conviction.

Of course there was more to the works of the court poets than mere ritual entertainment. As Peredur Lynch has ably demonstrated they were 'a learned order, whose rights and privileges were defined by law', so that they 'had a clear understanding of the intricacies of power and politics.'[37] Therefore, 'it can hardly be suggested that patronage in the poets' case was somehow enclosed in a sanitized cultural capsule and detached from an adulterating world of political scheming and empire-building.'[38] As propagandists they were vital cogs in the state-building activities of the princes but they also served their princes in more tangible and routine ways. For example, Meilyr Brydydd, court poet to Gruffudd ap Cynan, also served him as an emissary. Llywelyn too employed his poets as ministers and ambassadors; in 1223 he appointed Einion ap Gwalchmai to be one of a powerful group of negotiators tasked with defining the boundaries, both political and geographical, between the southern princelings. Clearly, these were men who stood tall in the service of their prince whom they served with conspicuous distinction.

By means of politics, patronage, propaganda and war,
Llywelyn had succeeded in creating a strong power-base in
Gwynedd from which to extend his sway in Wales. His military
power was used to conquer and then control those territories that
lay beyond the borders of Gwynedd. His soldiery and skill as a
strategist and tactician were impressive while his governance and
rulership were masterful. He was well represented by men,
clerical and lay, who were able to match the diplomatic skills of
the servants of other rulers. His munificent patronage earned him
plaudits from priests and poets and cemented his reputation as a
man of energy and vision.

Table 2: Llywelyn's Marriage Alliances

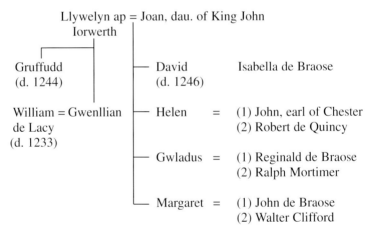

Llywelyn used his children to further state policy by carefully arranging
marriages in order to cement alliances with powerful Marcher families.

Notes

1. *Autobiog.*, 57.
2. BT.Pen., 102-3.
3. *Guide to Welsh Literature*, 153.
4. Ellis, T.P., *Welsh Tribal Law and Custom in the Middle Ages* (Oxford, 1926), 337.
5. Jones, G.R.J., 'The Defences of Gwynedd in the Thirteenth Century', *THSC* (1969), 34;
6. Carr, *MW*, 69.
7. Stephenson, *Governance of Gwynedd*, 24.
8. *BT.Pen*, 102.
9. Evans., *Mediaeval Prince*, 61.
10. Jack, R.I., *Medieval Wales* (London 1972), 200.
11. *Journey & Description*, 194.
12. Lloyd, *HW.*, II, 684.
13. *BT.Pen.*, 85.
14. *Ibid.*
15. Stephenson, *Governance of Gwynedd*, 7.
16. *Ibid.*
17. Pryce, Huw, *Native Law and the Church in Medieval Wales* (Oxford, 1993), 242.
18. *AWR.*, 414-5.
19. Davies, Rees, *et al.*, (eds.). *Welsh society and nationhood : historical essays presented to Glanmor Williams* (Cardiff, 1984), 55.
20. *Guide to Welsh Literature*, 179.
21. *Ancient Laws and Institutes of Wales*, ed. and trans. A. Owen (London, 1841), II, 381.
22. Davies, *Wales 1063-1415*, 254.
23. Williams, D.H., *Welsh History through Seals* (Cardiff, 1982), 19.
24. Costigan, N. G., *et al.* (eds.), *Gwaith Dafydd Benfras ac eraill o feirdd hanner cyntaf y drydedd ganrif ar ddeg* [The works of Dafydd Benfras and other thirteenth-century poets] (Cardiff, 1995), 33.
25. *AWR.*, 406.
26. Smith, *Llywelyn ap Gruffudd*, 20.
27. *AWR.*, 27-8.
28. Davies, *Wales 1063-1415*, 244.
29. *Ibid.*, 245.
30. Clanchy, M. T. *England and its rulers, 1066-1272* (2nd edn. Oxford, 1998), 180.
31. Carr, *MW.*, 66.
32. Bradbury, J., *Philip Augustus* (London, 1998), 21.
33. *Ibid.*, 22.
34. *Ibid.*, 23.
35. *BT.Pen.*, 105.
36. *AWR.*, 374.
37. Charles-Edwards, T.M. *et al.* (eds.), *The Welsh King and his Court* (Cardiff, 2000), 167.
38. *Ibid.*, 169.

VII

Pursuit of a Settlement:
Twilight Years and Death 1234-40

Well known it is that your long hand never falters
As it bestows the red and the yellow gold.
God made you braver than any man that breathes,
Most liberal, too, as far as the sun's course extends.
It is your father's kindly instinct that to you clings,
And in you the generous dead is reborn.[1]

[Llywarch ap Llywelyn (Prydydd Y Moch)]

Thus did the court poet Llywarch ap Llywelyn sing the praises of his master whom he regarded as the greatest prince of them all. Written some twenty years before Llywelyn's death, the poet did not witness his patron's inevitable decline into old age and death. Llywelyn's last years were marred by personal tragedy, family strife and debilitating illness but through it all he maintained his authority, dignity and reputation. Memorably described by David Carpenter as a 'flinty warrior, but also a sinuous politician',[2] Llywelyn's aim was to ensure the survival of his principality by means of the uncontested succession of his son. Realistically, the king of England alone had the power and authority to ensure the realisation of Llywelyn's aspirations. More in hope than in certainty, the prince devoted the remaining years of his life to converting his dream into reality. His task was clear: to bind the Crown into a formal agreement so that by means of the written word, Llywelyn might make his 'overlordship more precise, more vertebrate, more enduring.'[3]

THE PACT OF MYDDLE, 1234

In June 1234 Llywelyn's representative met the king's envoys in Shropshire at a place midway between the prince's manor of Ellesmere and Shrewsbury in order to conclude an agreement. The

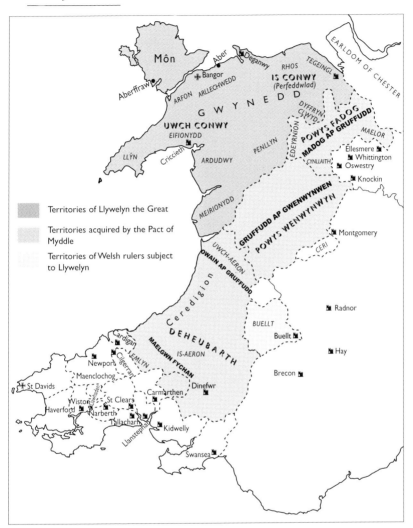

Wales in 1234: the extent of Llywelyn's territorial power towards the end of his reign.

so-called Pact of Myddle established a two-year truce and it was agreed that 'no new castle shall be fortified or demolished castle restored in the March during the truce.'⁴ In addition, all conquests of earlier date than the outbreak of the king's war with Earl Richard were to be retained, so that Llywelyn kept his hold on Cardigan and Builth. Llywelyn was equally delighted with the stripping of Peter de Rivallis of all his Welsh possessions. On the other hand, the entrusting of these lands to the new earl of Pembroke, Richard Marshal's brother, Gilbert, may have caused the prince some anxiety. For much of the thirteenth century, the Marshal family had been at odds with the prince of Gwynedd and their recent alliance notwithstanding, they soon returned to a state of mutual distrust and barely concealed hostility. Less than two years later, in 1236, the peace between them was shattered when Gilbert Marshal attacked and 'took by treachery' the castle of Machen, north of Cardiff, from Morgan ap Hywel. However, as the native chroniclers make clear, such was Llywelyn's power at this stage of his career that 'after making a great fortification around it he [Gilbert] gave back the castle for fear of the Lord Llywelyn.'[5]

Whether the Pact of Myddle can be considered, in the words of J.E. Lloyd, 'the crowning achievement of the prince's long and victorious career'[6] is a matter for debate. The pact was a truce rather than a peace treaty and its terms were provisional rather than permanent. On the other hand, the pact took on an air of permanence by the very fact that it was renewed from year to year until Llywelyn's death. True, Llywelyn 'fought no more battles with the English' and his confidence may be gauged by the release of his disaffected son, Gruffudd, from an imprisonment lasting six long years. However, we must be wary of attributing to this accord the status of a career-defining moment and it is surely too much to claim, as J.E. Lloyd did, that as a result Llywelyn 'had won for himself and for his people a secure and well-guarded independence.'[7] Less than seven years later, in 1241, that 'independence' looked anything but 'secure and well-guarded'. Much of what Llywelyn had achieved was lost by his son Dafydd when he was forced by Henry III to agree to the humiliating terms of the so-called Peace of Gwerneigron.

DYNASTIC SUCCESSION: DAFYDD VERSUS GRUFFUDD

In spite of its shortcomings, the Pact of Myddle, and the subsequent truces agreed with the Crown, did contribute to a stability of sorts in the remaining years of Llywelyn's reign.

Indeed, it is probably true to say that the history of Llywelyn from the Pact of Myddle until his death in 1240 is that of a prince who was supreme beyond challenge in his hereditary dominions and acknowledged overlord of those territories acquired through war and diplomacy. Only the spectre of family discord and possible civil war clouded what might otherwise have been a brilliant sunset in the great prince's career. Llywelyn pursued with ever-greater vigour his aim of securing the undisputed succession of his son Dafydd. The process had begun in 1220 when Henry III and his archbishop, Stephen Langton, formally acknowledged Dafydd, who was probably no more than five years old, as Llywelyn's heir to the exclusion of Gruffudd. Pope Honorious III followed this by confirming Dafydd's succession by hereditary right in 1222 and, in 1226, by legitimising Dafydd's mother Joan. Having secured the consent of the King of England, the Archbishop of Canterbury and the Pope, Llywelyn turned to the Welsh princes who were required, at a meeting held in 1226, to acknowledge Dafydd's succession and swear fealty to him.

Gruffudd was likely ten years or more older than his half-brother, Dafydd, so that his treatment at the hands of his father may have caused resentment and driven a wedge between them. In 1211 a young, probably teenage, Gruffudd was handed over by his father, as a pledge of the prince's good conduct, to King John who held him as a hostage for the next four years. When he returned to Gwynedd in 1215, Gruffudd became a thorn in his father's side and on each occasion they fell out, the tension between them increased. The cause of Gruffudd's imprisonment in Deganwy castle in 1228 and the confiscation of his lands – the cantref of Meirionnydd and commote of Ardudwy – is not known but it so closely corresponds in date to the resumption of hostilities between Llywelyn and the king that a link cannot be ruled out. Perhaps Llywelyn feared Gruffudd's defection to the English, as his uncle Dafydd had done more than thirty years earlier, in the hope that they might help him fulfil his dynastic hopes and ambitions. Llywelyn might have uncovered a plot involving rebellion or assassination of either himself or his heir.

Of course, Gruffudd may equally have been the victim of a plot to discredit him by rumour and false allegations. It is interesting to note that with Gruffudd safely imprisoned Llywelyn sought, in 1229, to secure the Crown's reaffirmation of its commitment to recognising Dafydd's succession

Whatever the reason for Gruffudd's incarceration, it was deemed necessary at the time and serious enough to last a considerable time. It was Gruffudd's misfortune to be illegitimate and be the half-brother of Dafydd, who was a grandson of a king of England, but whether he was as irresponsible and headstrong as T. Jones Pierce has suggested, is debatable. The sixteenth-century antiquary, Humphrey Llwyd, described Gruffudd as a 'lustie gentillman' but his opinion may have been coloured by the views of contemporary poets – Dafydd Benfras, Einion Wan and Einion ap Madog ap Rahawd – who praised his courage and warrior instincts. His father certainly trusted him enough to invest him with title to land within the kingdom and with the command of troops in war. In fact, the reconciliation effected between the two in 1234 was such that Gruffudd was immediately granted half of the lordship of Llŷn, to which was added over the next three years the other half of Llŷn and the whole of southern Powys. In granting Powys, first in 1226 but later withdrawn on his imprisonment, Llywelyn may have intended Gruffudd to be the successor of Gwenwynwyn to the permanent exclusion of the latter's sons.

The relationship between Gruffudd and Dafydd settled into an uneasy peace; neither was willing to reconcile entirely with the other. The tension caused by this familial enmity must have taken its toll on the ageing prince but it was likely the death of his wife of thirty-two years, in February 1237, which most affected his health. A short time later, according to Matthew Paris, Llywelyn suffered a paralytic stroke and although the extent of the disability is not known, it must have had a profound effect on him personally and on his position as prince. Fate played a cruel hand in 1237 when the prince's son-in-law, John the Scot, died without a male heir, which resulted in the earldom of Chester passing into the hands of the Crown. Thus, a reliable ally on his vulnerable eastern frontier had been replaced by a potential aggressor. To make matters worse, Gruffudd chose this moment to take up arms against his father in a last-ditch attempt either to improve his position in the kingdom or to remove his brother entirely. The rebellion failed but it convinced Llywelyn that more had to be done to secure Dafydd's succession.

Llywelyn's plan from the outset had been to encourage the Welsh princes to do homage and fealty to Dafydd by coercion if necessary. Late in 1237 in a meeting of the Welsh princes he set in motion the means whereby this could be effected. However, on hearing of Llywelyn's intentions in March 1238, the king issued a stream of letters addressed to the prince, his heir-designate, the Welsh princes and the Marcher lords. The king's concern is made manifest in those letters addressed to the Welsh princes, who were forcefully reminded that their homage was due to him alone and not to Llywelyn or his heir. At the same time Henry III summoned the Marcher lords to a meeting at Oxford to discuss the situation in Wales. Unfortunately, the outcome of their deliberations is not known. According to Matthew Paris, in a desperate attempt to enlist the support of the king, Llywelyn even contemplated putting his lands under the Crown's protection and, further, to consider offering military service. Both proposals would have served to undermine Llywelyn's quest for greater autonomy, but in the event nothing came of them. Nevertheless, as Rees Davies pointed out, 'such a recurrent search for assurances suggests that Llywelyn remained unconvinced that the arrangements would in fact survive him.'8

THE COUNCIL OF PRINCES AT STRATA FLORIDA, 1238

In October 1238, after months of preparation, an assembly of all the princes of Wales finally took place at the Cistercian abbey of Strata Florida. Mindful of the Crown's objection to the swearing of homage, Llywelyn backed down and required each of the princes to swear fealty to Dafydd as heir-apparent. This was no more than had been done in 1226 and it served as a reminder of that earlier pledge. However, if A.D. Carr is correct, this assembly might have served as an opportunity for Llywelyn effectively to abdicate and publicly invest his son with his princely powers: 'the object being to strengthen Dafydd's position in the face of an increasing threat from Gruffudd and his supporters'.[9] That he had not entirely divested himself of power may be gauged by a reference in the native chronicles which state that on hearing of the murder of Gruffudd Ial by his brother Maredudd ap Madog ap Gruffudd Maelor of Powys Fadog, Llywelyn immediately 'took from him all his territory'.[10] This was to be the last recorded act late in 1238 of a prince whose life and energies were slowly ebbing away.

Llywelyn had plainly failed in his bid to bind the princes to a firm contractual obligation and it would be left to Dafydd to establish his authority in native Wales. He began the task of exercising his power by stripping his half-brother of all his lands in Powys, leaving him only the lordship of Lleyn. By the summer of 1240, if not earlier, Llŷn, too, was taken by Dafydd from his brother whom he imprisoned, together with his son, Owain, in Cricieth castle. The means by which he effected his brother's capture, by tricking him into a meeting held under the protection of Richard, Bishop of Bangor, demonstrate Dafydd's firm grasp of the realities of dynastic politics. However, for this breach of faith, Dafydd earned the undying enmity of the bishop who retreated into exile rather than serve a duplicitous prince. Thus, within two years of the Strata Florida meeting, Dafydd had made himself undisputed master of Gwynedd; it remained to be seen whether he could fill his father's shoes by claiming, let alone exercising, his mastery over native Wales.

DEATH AND BURIAL

Possibly weary of life after long suffering the effects of ill-health, Llywelyn died on 11 April 1240; he was around sixty-seven years of age. He spent his last hours in the abbey of Aberconwy, where he took the monastic habit and where his body was honourably buried. That he chose not to be buried next to his wife need not

A section of text from the *Brut Y Tywysogyon* (Chronicles of the Princes) which refers to Dafydd imprisoning Gruffudd and his son at Cricieth in 1239.

(Peniarth MS 19, columns 639 and 640. National Library of Wales)

be taken as a sign of unrepaired relations after the Braose episode but rather as a concern to do right by his soul and the Cistercians to whom he had extended the generous hand of patronage.

Bard and chronicler sang his praises with a unanimous voice. In the opinion of the scribe responsible for compiling the *Annales Cambriae*, 'the lord Llywelyn son of Iorwerth son of Owain Gwynedd, then prince of Wales' was

> that great Achilles the second . . . whose deeds I am unworthy to recount. With lance and shield he tamed his foes; he maintained peace for the men of religion; to the poor he gave food and clothes. With a warlike cord he extended his boundaries; he showed good justice to all . . . and by bonds of fear or love bound all men to him.[11]

The poet Elidir Sais lamented the death of a prince with whom he had endured a strained relationship:

> I have seen Llywelyn, his hosts drawn from all parts of Wales;
> I have seen the leaders of Gwynedd and the South, pillars of war bivouacked together;
> I have seen men in battle and spirited horses, and wine, a following of people and jousting.
> I have seen hosts, daily carousals, and success upon success.
> That has all vanished like the drop of your hand, all have to leave this passing world.[12]

Elidir's poetic compatriot, Einion Wan, mourned the loss of an exceptional man:

> True lord of the land,
> How strange that to-day
> He rules not over Gwynedd
> Lord of nothing but the piled up stones of his tomb,
> The seven-foot grave in which he lies.[13]

Dafydd did not long mourn his father, for a little over a month later, on 15 May 1240, he was at Gloucester to meet King Henry III. Oaths of homage and fealty were demanded and duly given but Dafydd failed to persuade the king to recognise him as his father's heir in those lands that lay beyond Gwynedd. To the king, Dafydd was Prince of Gwynedd with no lawful claim to wider lordship. Unfortunately for Dafydd, his father's clients and allies deserted him in spite of their oaths to the contrary. Fifteen months later, in August 1241, war broke out but, unlike his father, Dafydd did not prosper. Isolated and overwhelmed by the forces arrayed against him, both English and Welsh, Dafydd had no choice but to surrender. In a peace treaty reminiscent of that imposed on his father by King John in 1211, Dafydd was stripped of his status and much of his territory and power. Worse, he faced the very real prospect of having to share Gwynedd with his half-brother, Gruffudd. Llywelyn's great legacy had been destroyed and the rights he had hoped to secure for his son had been lost in less than eighteen months.

Notes

1 Quoted in Lloyd, *HW*, II, 691.
2 Carpenter, *Britain 1066-1284*, 318.
3 Davies, R.R., *Domination and Conquest: the experience of Ireland, Scotland and Wales* (Cambridge, 1990), 96.
4 *AWR.*, 439.
5 *BT.Pen.*, 104.
6 Lloyd, *HW*, II, 681.
7 *Ibid.*
8 Davies, *Wales 1063-1415*, 249.
9 Carr, *NewDNB*, online edn.
10 *BT.Pen.*, 105.
11 *Annales Cambriae*, ed. J. Williams ab Ithel (Rolls Series, 1860), 82-3.
12 *Guide to Welsh Literature*, 177-8.
13 Lloyd, *HW*, II, 693.

VIII

'Lewelinus Magnus – Llywelyn Fawr': The Greatness of Llywelyn

> The thirteenth century may, in Welsh history, be appropriately described as the age of the two Llywelyns. During its first forty years the figure of the elder prince of that name mounts into ever-greater prominence until it dominates, in unquestioned pre-eminence, the whole of Wales.[1]

Thus did Sir John Edward Lloyd introduce Llywelyn ap Iorwerth to an unsuspecting pre-Great War audience. Lloyd's book was the first critical study of medieval Welsh history and though he wrote as a professional historian 'in accordance with modern standards of historical scholarship',[2] he could not resist expressing his native pride in a ruler of undoubted talent and singular ability. In Lloyd's certain opinion, Llywelyn's 'patriotic statesmanship will always entitle him to wear the proud style of Llywelyn the Great'.[3] How 'Great' Llywelyn is or was, is a matter for debate. Certainly, A.D. Carr, the most recent biographer of Llywelyn, seems not to share Lloyd's unrestrained admiration for a ruler who 'despite his achievements, might be said to have failed.'[4] The measure of Llywelyn's 'Greatness', lies somewhere between Lloyd and Carr for, in a career lasting more than forty years, he did indeed achieve a great deal but perhaps not as much as he might have done.

CONTEMPORARY ESTIMATION

As one might expect, the most fulsome praises of Llywelyn occur in the poems addressed to him by the court poets, chief among them Llywarch ap Llywelyn, Elidir Sais and Dafydd Benfras. All of them emphasized the fact that he possessed in abundance the military virtues deemed essential to any successful Welsh ruler of this period, and proclaimed that he was a worthy successor to earlier kings of Gwynedd such as Maelgwn and Rhodri Mawr. Elidir Sais likened Llywelyn to 'the Lord Caesar' because he was an 'excellent king' and 'a victorious hero', 'The Destroyer of England and destroyer of her people'.[5] Dafydd Benfras was almost lost for words in his extravagant eulogy:

> Had I the skill of a wizard
> In the primitive, eloquent bardic strain,
> I could not for the life of me paint his prowess in battle,
> Nor could Taliesin.[6]

To these eulogies could be added the praise poetry of equally skilled bards such as Einion ap Gwalchmai, Einion ap Gwgon, Einion Wan, Gwgon Brydydd and Llywelyn Fardd II. To them Llywelyn was undoubtedly a great man but they refrained from applying this particular epithet, preferring instead to praise his great deeds. For example, Dafydd Benfras called him the 'great head of Wales and its orderliness' and 'the ruler of rulers',[7] but he does not specifically refer to him as 'Great'.

It is easy to marginalise the bardic praise directed towards individual princes because it was in the stylized and ritualistic nature of the craft to be praiseworthy. Rarely did the bards criticise their patrons but when they did it is worth noting. Elidir Sais certainly angered Llywelyn, hence his retreat into exile for so long that he acquired the epithet 'Englishman'. He seemed ill at ease with Llywelyn's conquest of, and control over, the other Welsh princes:

> Think what you do when you commit aggression over a border, bringing everyone down to their knees. Be a supporter of the weak, be just and gentle to those of rightful descent, let there be mercy within your strongholds of stone, and the love of God.[8]

Even Llywarch ap Llywelyn, perhaps the most loyal of Llywelyn's poets, could speak plainly when roused to do so. In one poem he stood toe to toe with his prince, proclaiming 'Me – Llywarch; You – Llywelyn'.[9] He could be equally blunt with other patrons as in a poem, entitled *Bygwth Dafydd* (Threatening Dafydd) addressed to Llywelyn's uncle, in which he sang:

> You, ruler of the West, should do well by me;
> To insult me is to cast aspersions on my art.
> Better am I to you than many horses and their riders
> journeying afar on your errands.[10]

The court poets were well aware of their importance in terms of their propaganda value. Llywarch ap Llywelyn was never shy of proclaiming the 'inherent right' of a ruler of Aberffraw to claim leadership over native Wales. Indeed, unlike Elidir Sais, whom he criticised (among others) for expressing his disquiet over Llywelyn's claims to rule Wales, he gloried in his patron's disregard for frontiers. In one poem Llywarch appeals to the men of Powys not to oppose his master's lordship over them:

> Let the people of Powys realise who he is – the king of a strong people. Is it better to have a Frenchman than a passionate Welshman?[11]

Whether or not court poets like Llywarch ap Llywelyn can be credited with anticipating Llywelyn's 'policy of uniting as much of Wales as he could under his own rule', as suggested by D. Myrddin Lloyd, or of 'helping to create an attitude of mind conducive to the rise of a Llywelyn', is a matter for debate.[12] Nevertheless, it is true to say that to ignore the court poets or their bardic verse is a mistake, especially in respect of Llywelyn, for as the eminent historian Sir Rees Davies concluded, 'For once the plaudits of the bards were not exaggerating.'[13]

What is perhaps remarkable is the miserly praise, no more than a few lines, offered at his death by the various versions of the native chronicles. In the three editions of the *Brut y Tywysogyon* the chroniclers seemed at a loss as to how best to mark his passing, stating that though he was a 'second Achilles', he was a man for whom it was 'difficult for anyone to set forth his prowess and his deeds.'[14] The Latin versions of the native chroniclers, the *Annales*

Cambriae and *Cronica de Wallia,* are a little more fulsome in their praise but even they fall far short of the two-page encomium devoted to the Lord Rhys by the scribe responsible for the Peniarth version of the *Brut.* Whereas the Lord Rhys was lauded as 'the best that had ever been of the race of the Welsh',[15] Llywelyn had to be content with being a tamer of his foes, a maintainer of peace, a dispenser of justice and a giver of alms to the poor. This might reflect the way in which princes were being perceived by the middle decades of the thirteenth century surrounded by the trappings of bureaucracy rather than by warlike apparel. Their south–Wales bias notwithstanding, the native chroniclers might have been a little more forthcoming in praising Llywelyn given the fact that he looms large in their chronicles. That they found difficulty in expressing their admiration for him or felt unworthy to recount his achievements might suggest that while they acknowledged the significance of his reign, they lacked the understanding to assess properly the impact of his policies. As Rees Davies pointed out, 'There was a largeness of vision about his policies and methods unusual among Welsh princes – a readiness to appeal to the king and the papacy, to forge an alliance with the king of France, to counter threats of excommunication by an appeal to conscience and to God.'[16]

EVOLVING GREATNESS

If Welsh chroniclers were reluctant to celebrate the greatness of Llywelyn and the bards shy of applying the epithet 'Great', not so English monastic scribes and chancery clerks. Remarkably, the first to apply the epithet 'Great' to Llywelyn was the English cleric-chronicler, Matthew Paris. Writing from the summer of 1235 until his death in 1259, Paris was well placed to reflect on the achievements of a prince who was well known to his patron, Henry III. Indeed, it is probably from the king, as well as from others at court, that Paris probably derived much of his information on the Welshman. Writing of events in 1258, Paris makes reference to 'the sons of the great Llywelyn (*magni Lewelini*), whose many triumphs require to be particularly made mention of.'[17] Although he goes on to say that 'much has been previously said of him in this book in the proper place', it is in this instance only that the author passes judgement on Llywelyn. He may have done so out of a genuine sense of admiration for a ruler of exceptional ability or simply by comparison with Llywelyn's apparently less gifted sons and grandsons. That he had no love of the Welsh – they irritated him because of the regularity of their attacks on the border counties of England in search of plunder – adds to the objectivity of Paris's opinion. Indeed, unlike the court poets who were almost obliged to laud the greatness of their patron, whether or not this bore any relation to flawed reality, Paris was not so constrained.

No other chronicler of the thirteenth or succeeding century refers to Llywelyn as the Great in either Wales or England. However, although the original charter issued by Llywelyn to Beddgelert Priory has been lost, there is a reference in letters patent drawn up by Edward I's chancery clerks, dated May 1286, in which he is styled *Lewelini magnus*.[18] In translation this is usually taken to mean 'great' but it is inconceivable to think that English royal clerks would have ascribed an element of greatness to a long dead prince of a recently defeated people. If this was not written in error (and there is nothing to suggest that it was) then we may need to adjust our understanding of what some contemporaries meant by the term *magnus*. Among the first to question the meaning and use of *magnus* was the German historian, Michael Richter, who claimed, as far back as the late 1970s, that it might, in certain instances, mean 'the elder' rather than 'the great'.[19] He cited examples drawn from the native chronicles and from the charters of the princes of Deheubarth to show that the term was used to distinguish rulers with the same name from each other. Even Gerald of Wales's rendering of *Oeneus magnus* (Owain Gwynedd) should not, in Richter's opinion, have been translated by J.E. Lloyd as Owain 'the Great', but rather Owain 'the elder' in order to distinguish him from the other Owains who ruled at the same time, such as Owain Cyfeiliog and Owain ap Madog, both of Powys.

Thus, in Richter's opinion, 'the Welsh historian will have to learn also to speak of Llywelyn ap Iorwerth no longer as

Llywelyn Fawr but of Llywelyn the elder, if the thirteenth-century historians called him 'magnus' in order to distinguish him from Llywelyn ap Gruffudd.'[20] Richter's persuasive argument would certainly explain the use of the term by Edward I's clerks, but is less secure in explaining the meaning intended by Paris. Indeed, it should be remembered that 'elder' is comparative which *magnus* is not. Arguably, the chancery clerks aside, it is just as likely to denote some interpretation of greatness insofar as Gerald of Wales's description of Owain Gwynedd might have been intended to distinguish him as being the 'greater' or most powerful of the three like-named rulers in Wales. Whatever the truth of the matter, the fact remains that it is not until the sixteenth century that the issue of Llywelyn's reputation for greatness is addressed. The first in English to refer to Llywelyn as 'the Great' was, apparently, Dr. David Powel in his *Historie of Cambria now called Wales.*[21]

Published in 1584 at the behest of the Lord President of the Council of Wales, Sir Henry Sidney, Powel's *Historie* was the first printed history of Wales. Based largely, though not exclusively, on Humphrey Llwyd's *Cronica Walliae*, a translation of the *Brut y Tywysogyon*, which he completed in 1559, Powel's stated intention was to correct, augment and continue the *Cronica*. In the event, Powel did much more than that to the extent that his *Historie* is an almost entirely new book. Unlike Llwyd, Powel made use of English chroniclers like Matthew Paris and had access to official records courtesy of William Cecil, Lord Burghley. However, like Llwyd, Powel took the opportunity to express his own opinion and offer his own interpretation on events and people. For example, while Llwyd fully acknowledged Llywelyn to be a 'moste valyannte and noble prince' who 'often put his enymyes to flight, and defended his countrey, and augmented' it, and in spite of having 'governed Wales well and worthely' for nearly fifty years, he could not bring himself to describe the prince as 'Great'.[22]

Not so Powel, whose narrative of Llywelyn's exploits and his obvious admiration for the prince suggest that he fully intended his description of Llywelyn as *Leolinus Magnus* to mean 'the

Great' and not 'the elder'. This is perhaps not surprising given Powel's stated intention to counter 'the slanderous report of such writers, as in their books as do enforce everie thing that is done by the Welshmen to their discredit.'[23] Powel was in search of Welsh heroes, such as the fictional Madoc, supposedly an uncle of Llywelyn ap Iorwerth, who was credited with discovering America. Clearly, unlike Owain Glyndŵr who was abruptly dismissed as a rebel of little consequence, Llywelyn ap Iorwerth fitted Powel's concept of greatness and he did much to enhance and solidify the prince's historical reputation. The impact of Powel's *Historie* was immediate and lasting, being the 'authority' on which virtually all historians and writers of Welsh history depended until J.E. Lloyd's book of 1911.

Within a decade or two of Powel's publication, writers such as Sir John Wynn of Gwydir were almost self-consciously referring to Llywelyn as 'the Great or Prince Llywelyn'. In contrast to their north-Welsh counterparts, south Walians were slow to use the epithet 'Great' when referring to Llywelyn. For example, in manuscripts written between the last decade of the sixteenth century and the first two decades of the seventeenth, neither George Owen nor Sir James Perrot refers to Llywelyn as anything but the son of Iorwerth and as either king or prince of north Wales. By the eighteenth century there is no such reticence in describing Llywelyn as 'the Great', as may be evidenced in the works of Thomas Pennant, who was largely responsible for the rehabilitation of Glyndŵr's historical reputation, and Richard Fenton. Thus, by the eighteenth century, if not a little earlier, the epithet 'Great' had gained wider currency across Wales. Today, it is used almost without a second thought both by layman and historian alike. Whether or not Llywelyn deserves to be recalled as a great prince is another matter.

MODERN ESTIMATION

Modern historians appear not to share in the reticence displayed by their medieval annalistic predecessors. Writing at the beginning of the twentieth century, J.E. Lloyd left his readers in no doubt as to his opinion of Llywelyn, a man whose place among the princes of Wales 'will always be high, if not indeed the highest of all, for no man ever made better or more judicious use of the native force of the Welsh people for adequate national ends.'[24] In equating Llywelyn with the spirit of Welsh nationalism, Lloyd was reflecting the upsurge in national feeling and the consciousness of Wales as a nation and the Welsh as a people that were current at the time. It was an era of social and economic change, political action and cultural identity wrapped up in movements such as Cymru Fydd and Home Rule. Indeed, according to Gwyn Williams, even David Lloyd George was not averse to delving into Welsh history for his own political ends. During the 1890s he toured Wales giving lectures on 'Llywelyn the Great' whom he presented as an 'early apostle of Cymru Fydd'.[25]

For much of the next half-century Lloyd's History of Wales held the field but a new generation of historians came to the fore and their estimation of Llywelyn is altogether more measured. T. Jones Pierce did not view Llywelyn in the same nationalist context as Lloyd but concentrated instead on his statesmanship and leadership. To Jones Pierce, Llywelyn revealed his statesmanship in the way he attempted 'to conciliate his neighbours of the March' by means of marriage alliances. He was also willing to concede that Llywelyn was a 'great feudal magnate' who 'envisaged Wales as a feudal principality on the same model as the Scottish monarchy.' Indeed, Jones Pierce was of the certain opinion that Llywelyn 'during his closing years, was steadily shaping a constitutional policy of the kind brought to fruition by his grandson and namesake.'[26]

On the other hand, J. Beverley Smith is somewhat critical of those historians, like Lloyd, who suggest that it was Llywelyn's achievement, as opposed to that of his grandson, that should be 'considered to be the supreme accomplishment in the history of medieval Wales.'[27] As the author of a study of Llywelyn ap Gruffudd, he has demonstrated that his subject was every bit as talented, statesmanlike and charismatic as his grandfather and that 'one prince need not be diminished in order to respect another.'

In fact, Smith seems to share Lloyd's estimation of Llywelyn ap Iorwerth in whom was revealed the subtle blending of the qualities of the statesman with the invincible spirit of a leader in war, who combined the gift of opportunism with the prescience which ensured that the princely interest was never placed in jeopardy, and who skilfully steered his dominion through the vicissitudes of the early years to the security of the period of his maturity.[28]

Whilst acknowledging the primacy established by Llywelyn ap Gruffudd later in the thirteenth century, for Rees Davies, Llywelyn ap Iorwerth's achievement is arguably the more worthy:

> For forty years he had dominated the history of Wales . . . he had forged a measure of unity and purpose in native Wales such as it had not known hitherto. He was a man alive to the dignity of his status and the need to defend his pretensions at a theoretical level as well as pursue them by force.[29]

Despite Rees Davies's earnest hope that 'hindsight should not be summoned to belittle Llywelyn's achievements',[30] revisionism may yet tarnish Llywelyn's reputation. However, for the present, many historians would agree with A.D. Carr's summation that Llywelyn ap Iorwerth should be remembered as 'one of the greatest of all Welsh rulers' because 'having started from nothing, he ended his days as prince of Wales in all but name, having achieved this position entirely through his political and military ability.'[31]

Notes

1 Lloyd, *HW*, II, 612.
2 Carr, *MW*, 14.
3 Lloyd, *HW*, II, 693.
4 Carr, *NewDNB*, Online edn.
5 Translation by Einir Jones.
6 Lloyd, *HW*, II, 691.
7 *Guide to Welsh Literature*, 153, 184.
8 *Ibid., 177.*
9 *Ibid.*, 179.
10 *Ibid.*, 178.
11 Roderick, A.J. (ed.), *Wales Through the Ages* (2 vols., Cardiff, 1959-60), 102-3.
12 *Ibid.*, 103.
13 Davies, *Wales 1063-1415*, 251.
14 *B.Saes.*, 233.
15 *Ibid.*, 193.
16 Davies, *Wales 1063-1415*, 250.
17 Giles, *Matthew Paris*, II, 304.
18 *AWR.*, 347.
19 Richter, 'National Consciousness', 48.
20 *Ibid.*, 48-9.
21 Powel, D., *Historie of Cambria now called Wales (1584)*, 246.
22 Llwyd, *Cronica Walliae*, 206.
23 Carr, *MW*, 9.
24 Lloyd, *HW*, II, 693.
25 Williams, G.A., *When Was Wales?* (London, 1985), 230.
26 *DWB.*, 600.
27 Smith, *Llywelyn ap Gruffudd*, 3.
28 *Ibid.*, 3.
29 Davies, *Wales 1063-1415*, 250.
30 *Ibid.*, 251.
31 Carr, *NewDNB, online edn.*

BIBLIOGRAPHY

This book is based, as far as possible, on original sources most of them translated from Latin and Welsh. This is a highly selective and brief guide to works of use on the general topics covered by each of the chapters.

The Autobiography of Giraldus Cambrensis, ed. H.E. Butler (Rev.edn., Woodbridge, 2005).

Avent, Richard, *Cestyll Tywysogion Gwynedd: Castles of the princes of Gwynedd* (Cardiff, 1983).

Avent, Richard, 'Castles of the Welsh princes', *Château Gaillard*, 16 (1992).

Barbier, P., *The Age of Owain Gwynedd* (1908).

Benson, R.L. & Constable, G. (ed.), *Renaissance and Renewal in the Twelfth Century* (Oxford, 1982).

Binchy, D.A., *Celtic and Anglo-Saxon Kingship* (Oxford, 1970).

Binns, A., *Dedications to Monastic Houses in England and Wales* (Woodbridge, 1989).

Bramley, K.A., *et al.* (eds.). *Gwaith Llywelyn Fardd I ac eraill o feirdd y ddeuddegfed ganrif* [The works of Llywelyn Fardd and other twelfth-century poets] (Cardiff, 1994).

Carpenter, D.A., *The Reign of Henry III* (London, 1996).

Carpenter, D.A., *The Struggle for Mastery: Britain 1066-1284* (London, 2003).

Carr, A. D. 'Anglo-Welsh relations, 1066-1282', in Jones, M. C. E.; Vale, Malcolm Graham Allan (ed.), *England and her neighbours, 1066-1453: Essays in Honour of Pierre Chaplais* (London, 1989), 121-38.

Carr, A.D., *Llywelyn ap Gruffudd* (Cardiff, 1982).

Carr, A.D., *Medieval Wales* (London, 1995).

Carr, A.D., 'Llywelyn ap Iorwerth', *New Oxford Dictionary of National Biography*, online edition.

Church, S. D. (ed.), *King John : new interpretations* (Woodbridge, 1999).

Costigan, N. G., *et al.* (eds.), *Gwaith Dafydd Benfras ac eraill o feirdd hanner cyntaf y drydedd ganrif ar ddeg* [The works of Dafydd Benfras and other thirteenth-century poets] (Cardiff, 1995).

Cowley, F.G., *The Monastic Order in South Wales, 1066-1349* (Cardiff, 1977).

Crouch, David B., *William Marshal : court, career and chivalry in the Angevin Empire, 1147-1219* (London, 1990).

Crouch, David B., *The Image of Aristocracy in Britain 1000-1300* (London, 1992).

Davies, R.R., *Conquest, Coexistence and Change Wales 1063-1415* (Oxford, 1987). [paperback edition entitled *Age of Conquest: Wales, 1063-1415* (Oxford, 1990).]

Davies, R.R. (ed.), *The British Isles, 1150-1500: Comparisons, Contrasts and Connections* (Edinburgh, 1988).

Davies, R.R., *Domination and Conquest: the experience of Ireland, Scotland and Wales* (Cambridge, 1990).

Davies, Sean. *Welsh Military Institutions, 633-1283* (Cardiff, 2004).

Davies, W.E., *Wales in the Early Middle Ages* (Leicester, 1982).

Charles-Edwards, T.M., 'The Heir-Apparent in Irish and Welsh Law', *Celtica*, IX, 180-90.

Charles-Edwards, T.M. et al. (eds.), *The Welsh King and his Court* (Cardiff, 2000).

Edwards, J.G., 'The Royal Household in the Welsh Lawbooks', *TRHS*, XIII (1963), 163-76.

Giles, J. A. (transcr.), *Matthew Paris's English history (with a continuation) from 1235 to 1273* (3 vols., London, 1852-4).

Hallam, E., 'Royal Burial and Cult of Kingship in Medieval England, 1060-1330', *Journal of Medieval History*, 8 (1982), 359-80.

Holden, Brock W., 'King John, the Braoses, and the Celtic fringe, 1207-1216', *Albion*, 33:1 (2001), 1-23.

Howell, M., 'Regalian Rights in Wales and the March: the Relation of Theory to Practice', *WHR*, VII (1975), 269-88.

Insley, Charles, 'From *Rex Wallie* to *Princeps Wallie* : charters and state formation in thirteenth-century Wales', in Maddicott, J. R.; Palliser, David Michael (ed.), *The Medieval State: Essays Presented to James Campbell* (London, 2000), 179-96.

Insley, Charles, 'The wilderness years of Llywelyn the Great', in Prestwich, Michael; Britnell, Richard Hugh; Frame, Robin (ed.), *Thirteenth-Century England IX: Proceedings of the Durhan Conference, 2001* (Woodbridge, 2003), 163-73.

Jack, R.I., *Medieval Wales* (London, 1972).

Jarman, A.O.H & Hughes, G.R. (eds.), *A Guide to Welsh Literature* (2 vols., Swansea, 1976; repr., 1979).

Jenkins, D., 'Cynghellor and Chancellor', *BBCS*, XXVII (1976), 115-18.

Jenkins, D., 'Kings, Lords and Princes: the Nomenclature of Authority in Thirteenth-Century Wales', *BBCS*, XXVI (1976), 451-62.

Jolliffe, J.E.A., *Angevin Kingship* (London, 1963).

Jones, G.R.J., 'The Defences of Gwynedd in the Thirteenth Century', *THSC*, (1969), 29-43.

Jones, N.A. & Pryce, H., *Yr Arglwydd Rhys* (Cerdydd, 1996).

Jones, Thomas (ed.), *Brut y Tywysogyon, or, Chronicle of the Princes: Peniarth MS 20 version* (Cardiff, 1952).

King, D.J.C., *Castellarium Anglicanum: An Index and Bibliography of Castles in England* (1983).

Knowles, D. & Hadcock, R.N., *Medieval Religious Houses. England and Wales* (2nd. edn., London, 1971).

Koch, J.T., 'When was Welsh Literature first written down?', *Studia Celtica*, XX/XXI (1985-6), 43-66.

Lewis, C.W., 'The Treaty of Woodstock, 1247: its backgound and significance', *WHR*, II (1964), 37-65.

Lloyd, J.E., *A History of Wales from earliest times to the Edwardian Conquest* (2 vols., London, 1911).

Llwyd, Humphrey, *Cronica Walliae*, ed. Ieuan M. Williams (Cardiff, 2002).

Maud, R., 'David, the last prince of Wales', *THSC* (1968), 43-62.

Maund, K.L. (ed.), *Gruffudd ap Cynan: a collaborative biography* (Woodbridge, 1996).

Maund, K.L., *Handlist of the acts of native Welsh rulers, 1132-1283* (Cardiff, 1996).

Maund, K.L., *The Welsh Kings* (Stroud, 2000).

Pierce, T.J., *Medieval Welsh Society*, ed. J.B. Smith (Cardiff, 1972).

Pryce, Huw, *Native law and the church in medieval Wales* (Oxford, 1993).

Pryce, Huw (ed.). *The Acts of Welsh Rulers, 1120-1283* (Cardiff, 2005).

Pryce, Huw, 'Owain Gwynedd and Louis VII: The Franco-Welsh Diplomacy of the First Prince of Wales', *WHR*, XIX (1998), 1-28.

Pryce, Huw. 'Negotiating Anglo-Welsh relations: Llywelyn the Great and Henry III', in Weiler, Björn K. U.; Rowlands, Ifor W. (ed.), *England and Europe in the Reign of Henry III (1216-1272)* (Aldershot, 2002), 13-29.

Pryce, Huw. 'Culture, power and the charters of Welsh rulers', in Flanagan, Marie Therese; Green, Judith A. (ed.), *Charters and*

Charter Scholarship in Britain and Ireland (Basingstoke, 2005), 184-202.

Richter, M., 'David ap Llywelyn, the first prince of Wales', *WHR*, V (1970-1), 205-19.

Richter, M., 'The Political and Institutional background to National Consciousness in Medieval Wales', in Moody, T.W. (ed.), *Nationality and the Pursuit of National Independence* (Belfast, 1978), 37-55.

Roderick, A.J., 'The Feudal Relations between the English Crown and the Welsh Princes', *History*, XXXVII (1952), 210-12.

Roderick, A.J., 'Marriage and Politics in Wales, 1066-1282', *WHR*, IV (1968-9), 1-20.

Rowlands, I.W., 'King John and Wales', in Church, S. D. (ed.). *King John : new interpretations* (Woodbridge, 1999), 273-87.

Rowlands, I. W., 'The 1201 peace between King John and Llywelyn ap Iorwerth'. *Studia Celtica*, 34 (2000), 149-66.

Smith, J.B., *Llywelyn ap Gruffudd Prince of Wales* (Cardiff, 1998).

Smith, J. B., Smith, L.B. (ed.). *History of Merioneth, volume II : The middle ages* (Cardiff, 2001).

Smith, J.B., 'Offra Principis Wallie Domino Regi', *BBCS*, XXIV (1966), 362-7.

Smith, J.B., 'Owain Gwynedd', *TCHS*, 32 (1971), 8-17.

Smith, J.B., 'The Treaty of Lambeth, 1217', *EHR*, 94 (1979), 562-79.

Smith, J.B., 'Magna Carta and the Charters of the Welsh Princes', *EHR*, 99 (1984), 344-62.

Stephenson, D., *The Governance of Gwynedd* (Cardiff, 1984).

Treharne, R.F., 'The Franco-Welsh Treaty of alliance in 1212', *BBCS*, XVIII (1958), 60-75.

Turvey, R.K., *The Lord Rhys Prince of Deheubarth* (Llandysul, 1997).

Turvey, R.K., *The Welsh Princes, 1063-1283* (London, 2002).

Walker, D.G., *The Norman Conquerors* (Swansea, 1977).

Walker, D.G. (ed.), *A History of the Church in Wales* (Penarth, 1976; repr. 1991).

Walker, D.G., *Medieval Wales* (Cambridge, 1990; repr., 1994).

Walker, R. F., 'Hubert de Burgh and Wales, 1218-32', *EHR* 87 (1972), 465-94.

Warren, W.L., *King John* (2nd. Edn., London, 1978).

Williams, J.E.C., *The Poets of the Welsh Princes* (Cardiff, 1978).

Williams, G., *Welsh Poetry, Sixth Century to 1600* (Cardiff, 1973).

Williams, G.A., 'The Succession to Gwynedd, 1238-1247', *BBCS*, XX (1962-64), 393-413.

Williams, G.A., *The Welsh in their History* (London, 1982).

Williams, G.A., *When Was Wales?* (London, 1985).

Wynn, John, Sir. *The History of the Gwydir Family, and Memoirs*, ed. Jones, J.G. (Llandysul, 1990).

INDEX